A LITTLE MATH WITH YOUR BUSINESS

Second Edition

Robert A. Brechner
Miami-Dade Community College

Introduction to Business Program

Louis E. Boone
University of South Alabama

David L. Kurtz
University of Arkansas

The Dryden Press
Harcourt Brace College Publishers

Fort Worth   Philadelphia   San Diego   New York   Orlando   Austin   San Antonio
Toronto   Montreal   London   Sydney   Tokyo

Address for Orders
The Dryden Press
6277 Sea Harbor Drive
Orlando, FL 32887-6777
1-800-782-4479 or 1-800-433-0001 (in Florida)

Address for Editorial Correspondence
The Dryden Press
301 Commerce Street, Suite 3700
Fort Worth, TX 76102

ISBN: 0-03-017807-X

Printed in the United States of America

5 6 7 8 9 0 1 2 3 4   095   9 8 7 6 5 4 3 2 1

The Dryden Press
Harcourt Brace College Publishers

In memory of

NATHAN BRECHNER

My Mentor, My Inspiration,
My Pal, My Dad

PREFACE

TO THE STUDENT

Mathematics in business is like a shadow, extremely hard to get away from! *A Little Math With Your Business* is a self-paced workbook, designed to provide beginning business students with some first-hand experience in solving basic business-related math problems.

The supplement has three main objectives: (1) to provide you with a business-oriented review of the basic arithmetic operations, (2) to provide a preview of some of the math you will encounter in such courses as business math, accounting, finance, marketing, and statistics, and (3) to serve, in the future, as a bookshelf reference of commonly used formulas, tables, conversions, terminology, and procedures related to business math.

The problems in this supplement cover a wide variety of math applications from today's dynamic business environment, with particular emphasis on entry-level management situations. Each section contains a multitude of hypothetical business problems. Some of the areas covered are:

Checking Accounts
Revenue, Expenses, and Profit
Stock Transactions, Profit and Loss
Employee Compensation and Payroll
Markup and Markdown
Sales and Property Tax
Expense Estimates
Market Share
Inventory
Depreciation
Distribution of Overhead
Production Capacities and Output
Quality Control
Warehousing and Transportation

HOW THE SUPPLEMENT IS ORGANIZED

A Little Math with Your Business is divided into four sections and an appendix. Section I, Basic Business Calculations, is intended as a review of the arithmetic operations: whole numbers, fractions, and decimals. For each of these operations, the review consists of a 20-30 question **Assessment Exercise** and a **Review Chart.** At the end of this and the other sections is an **Assessment Test,** which is used to measure your comprehension of the material.

The next three sections are designed to help you in your study by presenting the topics in small, easy-to-comprehend amounts, with frequent checks to determine whether you fully understand the material. As you progress through these sections, you will read an explanation of a concept and be given an **Example** along with a detailed **Solution Strategy.** You will then complete a few **Try-It Exercises.** The answers and worked-out solutions to the Try-Its are in the appendix. More detailed instructions for using the supplement can be found at the beginning of Section I.

Section II, Percents and Their Application in Business, introduces you to the commonly used concept of percents in business. This important topic is covered in considerable detail, with many Try-It Exercises for you to use in sharpening your skills with percents.

Section III, Business Statistics and Data Presentation, presents you with some of the basic topics of business statistics, such as averages. In this section, you will not only learn to read and interpret graphs, charts, and tables, but also to create these widely-used business communications tools.

Section IV, Business Measurements, Currency Conversion, and the Metric System, will take you on a mathematical journey through the various measurements and conversions of the familiar U. S. Customary System, and the "not so familiar" Metric System. In addition, you will learn to convert the major currencies of the world as you hypothetically conduct business in the global marketplace.

The Appendix contains three parts: Answers, Worked-out Solutions, and a business math glossary called **Glossary**^PLUS. The **Answers** section should be used to compare your answers to the Assessment and Try-It Exercises with the correct ones. The **Worked-out Solutions** section should only be consulted <u>after</u> you have made a second attempt to solve the problem without getting the right answer.

The **Glossary**^PLUS is a comprehensive listing of important business math terminology. Wherever applicable, the definitions are followed by the formula used to calculate that term. For students of business administration, this glossary, as well as the formulas, charts, and conversion tables, was designed to be used as a "bookshelf reference" long after the course has ended. Keep this supplement, along with your dictionary, thesaurus, and other reference books, in a convenient place where you study.

HOW TO GET THE MOST OUT OF THIS SUPPLEMENT

Maximum value will be derived from this supplement if you approach it as a learning opportunity and a challenge, not simply another homework assignment. The object is to work your way through each section and part of the supplement; checking your progress and correcting your mistakes. You should work at your own pace, making every effort to understand the concepts being presented. Except for the Assessment Tests, you are encouraged to work with a "study companion." No doubt, each of you will contribute something to the other's understanding of the material. After all, two heads are better than one!

You are not necessarily expected to fully understand each concept being presented. If after a diligent effort, you still don't understand certain topics, skip them and move on to the next. Remember, this supplement is meant to be a "preview" of things to come. After you complete all of the sections, you should have a pretty fair indication of your strengths and weaknesses in the area of basic business math.

You will need a calculator with which you are familiar and comfortable to assist you in working the problems. If you don't already have a calculator, now is the time to buy one. There is no need to spend a lot of money; any simple four-function calculator with memory will do. Be sure that you purchase one with an easy to read eight-place display and a keypad large enough to use for extended periods of time.

ACKNOWLEDGMENTS

I would like to thank the staff at The Dryden Press for their encouragement and professional help in making this supplement a reality. Particular thanks go out to Diana Farrell, publisher; Daryl Fox, my acquisitions editor; Stacey Sims my developmental editor; and Lisé Johnson, Marketing Manager.

Source: CALVIN AND HOBBES copyright 1992 Watterson. Dist. by UNIVERSAL PRESS SYNDICATE. Reprinted with permission. All rights reserved.

A LITTLE MATH
WITH
YOUR BUSINESS

TABLE OF CONTENTS

APPENDIX   113

Section I

Basic
Business
Calculations

$+$ $-$

$\times$ $\div$

2/3   \$1.49   3/4

SECTION I

BASIC BUSINESS CALCULATIONS

INSTRUCTIONS

Section I, Basic Business Calculations, is designed to evaluate your current math ability in the areas of whole numbers, fractions, and decimals. This section contains Assessment Exercises for each of these areas, as well as Summary Charts for a "quick reference" review.

"No Math Anxiety Permitted!!" These exercises are not tests; they are "self-evaluation" tools that you should use to identify your strengths and weaknesses in the basic arithmetic operations used in business. Before attempting the Assessment Exercises, look over the summary charts. These will give you a preview of the procedures in each exercise. If they seem basic to you, go on to the Assessment Exercises. If not, look them over more closely; reading each "Important Concept" and step-by-step "Illustrative Example."

Each Assessment Exercise is divided into two groups of questions: basic math operations and business-oriented word problems. The **basic math** operations should be worked first—by hand, with pencil and paper. Take your time, verify your work, and strive for accuracy. If there are any procedures you have forgotten, or don't understand, skip them for now.

The business **word problems** should be worked with a calculator. These problems ask you to apply basic arithmetic operations in business-related problems. Here you will have the opportunity to "think through" and solve some common business math problems. Again, skip any questions you don't understand. These will be clarified later with "worked-out solutions."

There is no time limit for completing these exercises. Work at your own pace, in a quiet, comfortable place. When you have completed Assessment Exercise #1, Whole Numbers, check your answers with the correct answers in the appendix. For each incorrect answer in the **basic math** section, locate the question number in the A/E# column of the Summary Chart and read the explanation of the correct procedure. Now, try to work the problem again.

For each incorrect answer in the **word problem** section, try once again. If you still don't get the answer, check the "worked-out solutions" listed after the answers. Repeat this process for Assessment Exercise #2, Fractions, and Assessment Exercise #3, Decimals.

After completing all three Assessment Exercises, and correcting your errors using the Summary Charts and the Worked-out solutions, you will have reviewed many of the basic math skills required in business today. When you feel confident about your performance and your corrected answers, go on to the Section I Assessment Test.

Whole Numbers
Summary Chart

Topic	A/E#	Important Concepts	Illustrative Examples
Reading and Writing Whole Numbers	1-2-3-4	1. Insert the commas every 3 digits, to mark the groups, beginning at the right side of the number. 2. Begin from left to right, naming the digits and the groups. Units, the only exception, are not named, and groups that have all zeros are not named. 3. when writing whole numbers in word form, the numbers from 21 to 99 are hyphenated. **Note:** The word "and" should <u>not</u> be used in reading or writing whole numbers.	The number 15538 takes on the numerical form "15,538" and is read, "fifteen thousand, five hundred thirty-eight." The number 22939643 takes on the numerical form "22,939,643" and is read, "twenty-two million, nine hundred thirty-nine thousand, six hundred forty-three." The number 1000022 takes on the numerical value "1,000,022" and is read one million twenty-two "
Rounding Whole Numbers to a Specified Place Value and All the Way	5-6-7	1. Determine the place to which the number is to be rounded. 2a. If the digit to the right of the one being rounded is 5 or more, increase the digit in the place being rounded by 1. 2b. If the digit to the right of the one being rounded is 4 or less, do not change the digit in the place being rounded. 3. Change all digits to the right of the place being rounded to zeros.	1,449 rounded to **tens** = 1,450 255 rounded to **hundreds** = 300 345,391 rounded to **thousands** = 345,000 768,892 rounded **all the way** = 800,000 68,658,000 rounded to **millions** = 69,000,000
Addition of Whole Numbers	8-12-13-14-16-17	1.Write the whole numbers in columns so that you line up the place values, units, tens, hundreds, etc. 2. Add the digits in each column, starting on the right with the units column. 3. When the total in a column is greater than 9, write the units digit and "carry" the tens digit to the top of the next column to the left. To **verify** your addition, add the numbers in reverse, from bottom to top.	211 1,931 **addend** 2,928 **addend** +5,857 **addend** 10,716 **sum**

Subtraction of Whole Numbers	9-12-14-15-19-20	1. Write the whole numbers in columns so that you line up the place values. 2. Starting with the units column, subtract the digits. 3. When a column can't be subtracted, you must **"borrow"** a digit from the column to the left of the one you are working in. **Note:** Since each place value increases by a factor of "ten times" as we move from right to left (units, tens, hundreds, etc.), when we "borrow" a digit, we are actually borrowing a "10." To **verify** your subtraction, add the difference and the subtrahend. This should equal the minuend.	$\begin{array}{ll} 34{,}557 & \textbf{minuend} \\ -\,6{,}224 & \textbf{subtrahend} \\ \hline 28{,}333 & \textbf{difference} \end{array}$ **Verification:** $\begin{array}{l} 28{,}333 \\ +\,6{,}224 \\ \hline 34{,}557 \end{array}$
Multiplication of Whole Numbers	10-13-16-17-18-20	1. Write the multiplication factors in columns so that the place values are lined up: units, tens, hundreds, etc. 2. Multiply each digit of the multiplier, starting with units, times the multiplicand. Each will yield a partial product whose units digit appears under the corresponding digit of the multiplier. 3. Add the digits in each column of the partial products, starting on the right, with the units column. To **verify** multiplication, divide the product by the multiplier. This should yield the multiplicand.	$\begin{array}{ll} 258 & \textbf{multiplicand} \text{ or factor} \\ \times\,43 & \textbf{multiplier} \text{ or factor} \\ \hline 774 & \text{partial product 1} \\ 1032 & \text{partial product 2} \\ \hline 11094 & \textbf{product} \end{array}$ **Verification:** $\dfrac{11094}{43} = 258$
Division of Whole Numbers	11-17-19	1. The number being divided is the **dividend.** The number by which we are dividing is the **divisor.** The answer is known as the **quotient.** 2. If the divisor does not divide evenly into the dividend, the quotient will have a **remainder.** To **verify** division, multiply the divisor by the quotient and add the remainder. This should yield the dividend.	$650 \div 27 = \dfrac{650}{27} =$ $\begin{array}{r} 24 \text{ R } 2 \\ 27\overline{)650} \\ \underline{54} \\ 110 \\ \underline{108} \\ 2 \end{array}$ **Verification:** $27 \times 24 = 648 + 2 = 650$

ASSESSMENT EXERCISE #1
Whole Numbers

Read and write the following whole numbers in numerical and word form:

	Number	Numerical Form	Word Form
1.	200049	_____	_____
2.	12308411	_____	_____

Write the following whole numbers in numerical form:

3. Three hundred sixteen thousand, two hundred twenty-nine _____

4. Four million, five hundred sixty thousand _____

Round the following numbers to the indicated place:

5. 18,334 to hundreds _____

6. 3,545,687 all the way _____

7. 256,733 to ten thousands _____

Perform the indicated operation:

8. 56,590 + 4,533 + 94 + 2,300,898 _____

9. 132,219 − 54,622 _____

10. 2,002 × 844 _____

11. 2,380 ÷ 140 _____

12.   The following chart shows Melody Music Shop's item sales breakdown for last week. Fill in all the blank spaces, and calculate the week's grand total?

	Monday	Tuesday	Wednesday	Thursday	Friday	Saturday	Total Units
Records	82	_____	68	57	72	92	_427_
Tapes	29	69	61	_____	82	75	_____
CDs	96	103	71	108	112	159	_____
Daily Totals	_____	_____	_____	_223_	_____	_____	_____

Using a calculator, solve the following word problems:

13.   You are the bookkeeper for Melody Music Shop in problem 12 above. Your boss just asked you for the dollar sales total for last week. Records sell for $9 each, tapes sell for $6 each, and CDs sell for $13 each.

14.   Nina Sanders had $868 in her checking account on April 1. During the month she wrote checks for $15, $123, $88, $276, and $34. She also deposited $45, $190, and $436. What is the balance in Nina's checking account at the end of April?

15.   A company projected profits to be $2,890,000. If actual profits were $3,009,770, by how much was the projection under the actual profits?

16.   Jeffrey Miller makes a salary of $23,440 per year, plus a commission of $300 per month. What is his weekly income?

17. You are in charge of putting together the annual "Stockholders Luncheon" for your company. The meal will cost $13 per person; entertainment will cost $2,100; facility rental amounts to $880; invitations and annual report printing costs amount to $2,636; other expenses come to $1,629. If 315 stockholders plan to attend,

   A. What is the total cost of the affair?

   B. What is the cost per stockholder?

18. Century Bank requires mortgage loan applicants to have monthly income of 5 times the amount of their monthly payment. How much monthly income must Jennifer Adams make in order to qualify for a payment of $565?

19. The Wilsons purchased a home for $165,000. They made a $45,600 down payment and will pay the owner equal monthly payments with no interest.

   A. How much will the monthly payments be if the Wilsons want to pay off the loan in 2 years?

   B. How much will the payments be if the loan was extended for 5 years?

20. Star-Bright Security charges $14 per hour for security guards. They pay the guards $8 per hour. If Star-Bright has 30 guards, each working a 25 hour week, how much profit did the company make last week?

Fractions
Summary Chart

Topic	A/E#	Important Concepts	Illustrative Examples
Terminology and Types of Fractions	1-2-3	**Common or Proper Fraction:** A fraction representing less than a "whole" unit, where the numerator is less than the denominator. **Improper Fraction:** A fraction representing one "whole" unit or more, where the denominator is equal to or less than the numerator. **Mixed Number:** A number that combines a whole number with a proper fraction.	$\dfrac{4}{7}$, $\dfrac{2}{3}$, $\dfrac{93}{124}$ $\begin{array}{l}\to \textbf{Numerator}\\ \to \textbf{Divided By}\\ \to \textbf{Denominator}\end{array}$ $\dfrac{5}{4}$, $\dfrac{7}{7}$, $\dfrac{88}{51}$, $\dfrac{796}{212}$, $\dfrac{1,200}{1,200}$ $12\dfrac{2}{5}$, $4\dfrac{5}{9}$, $78\dfrac{52}{63}$
Converting Improper Fractions to Whole or Mixed Numbers	4-5	1. Divide the numerator of the improper fraction by the denominator. 2a. If there is no remainder, the improper fraction becomes a whole number. 2b. If there is a remainder, write the whole number and then write the fraction as: whole number $\dfrac{\text{remainder}}{\text{divisor}}$	$\dfrac{68}{4} = 17$ $\dfrac{127}{20} = 6\dfrac{7}{20}$
Converting Mixed Numbers to Improper Fractions	6-7	1. Multiply the denominator by the whole number. 2. Add the numerator to the product from step 1. 3. Place the total from step 2 as the "new" numerator. 4. Place the original denominator as the "new" denominator.	$15\dfrac{3}{4} = \dfrac{(15 \times 4) + 3}{4} = \dfrac{63}{4}$
Reducing Fractions to Lowest Terms by Inspection	8-9	Reducing a fraction means finding whole numbers, called **common divisors** or **common factors,** which divide evenly into both the numerator and denominator of the fraction. When a fraction has been reduced to the point where there are no common divisors left, other than 1, it is said to be **reduced to lowest terms.**	$\dfrac{24}{120} = \dfrac{24 \div 3}{120 \div 3} = \dfrac{8}{40}$ $\dfrac{8}{40} = \dfrac{8 \div 2}{40 \div 2} = \dfrac{4}{20}$ $\dfrac{4}{20} = \dfrac{4 \div 4}{20 \div 4} = \dfrac{1}{5}$

Finding the Greatest Common Divisor (Reducing Shortcut)	8-9	The largest number that is a common divisor of a fraction is known as the **greatest common divisor** (GCD). It reduces the fraction to lowest terms in one step. To find the **GCD:** 1. Divide the numerator of the fraction into the denominator. 2. Take the remainder from step 1 and divide it into the divisor from step 1. 3. Repeat this division process until the remainder is either 0 or 1. If the remainder is 0, the last divisor is the greatest common divisor. If the remainder is 1, the fraction cannot be reduced, and is therefore in its lowest terms.	What greatest common divisor will reduce the fraction 48/72? $$48\overline{\smash{)}72}^{\,1}$$ $$\underline{48}$$ $$24$$ $$24\overline{\smash{)}48}^{\,2}$$ $$\underline{48}$$ $$0$$ The greatest common divisor is <u>24</u>
Raising Fractions to Higher Terms	10-11	To raise a fraction to a new denominator: 1. Divide the original denominator into the new denominator. The resulting quotient is the common multiple, which raises the fraction. 2. Multiply the numerator and the denominator of the original fraction by the common multiple.	Raise 5/8 to forty-eighths: $$\frac{5}{8} = \frac{?}{48}$$ $$48 \div 8 = 6$$ $$\frac{5 \times 6}{8 \times 6} = \frac{30}{48}$$
Prime Numbers	12	A **prime number** is a whole number, greater than 1, which is divisible only by 1 and itself. They are used to find the least common denominator.	Examples of **prime numbers:** 2, 3, 5, 7, 11, 13, 17, 19, 23, 29
Determining the Least Common Denominator, LCD, of Two or More Numbers.	12	1. Write all the denominators in a row. 2. Find the smallest prime number that divides evenly into any of the denominators. Write that prime number to the left of the row, and divide. Place all quotients and undivided numbers in the next row down. 3. Repeat this process until the new row contains all ones. 4. Multiply all the prime numbers on the left together, to get the LCD of the fractions.	Determine the LCD of 2/9, 5/6, 1/4, and 4/5 <u>Prime Number</u> <u>Denominators</u> 3 <u>9</u> <u>6</u> <u>4</u> <u>5</u> 2 <u>3</u> <u>2</u> <u>4</u> <u>5</u> 2 <u>3</u> <u>1</u> <u>2</u> <u>5</u> 3 <u>3</u> <u>1</u> <u>1</u> <u>5</u> 5 <u>1</u> <u>1</u> <u>1</u> <u>5</u> 1 1 1 1 **LCD** = 3 x 2 x 2 x 3 x 5 = <u>180</u>

Adding Proper Fractions with Like Denominators		1. Add all the numerators and place the total over the original denominator 2. If the result is a proper fraction, reduce it to lowest terms. 3. If the result is an improper fraction, convert it to a whole or a mixed number.	Add: $\frac{8}{9}$, $\frac{4}{9}$, and $\frac{1}{9}$ $\frac{8+4+1}{9} = \frac{13}{9} = 1\frac{4}{9}$
Adding Proper Fractions with Different Denominators	14	1. Find the least common denominator of the unlike fractions. 2. Raise each fraction to the terms of the LCD, thereby making them like fractions. 3. Now follow the same procedure used for adding like fractions.	Add: $\frac{2}{3} + \frac{5}{7}$ $LCD = 3 \times 7 - 21$ $\frac{2 \times 7}{21} + \frac{5 \times 3}{21} = \frac{14+15}{21} = \frac{29}{21} =$ $1\frac{8}{21}$
Adding Mixed Numbers	18-21	1. Add the whole numbers. 2. Add the fractions, and reduce to lowest terms. If they are improper, convert to whole or mixed numbers. 3. Add the whole numbers from step 1, and the fractions from step 2, to get the total.	Add: $3\frac{3}{4} + 4\frac{1}{8}$ $3 + 4 = 7$ $\frac{3}{4} + \frac{1}{8} = \frac{(3 \times 2)+1}{8} = \frac{7}{8}$ $7 + \frac{7}{8} = 7\frac{7}{8}$
Subtracting Proper Fractions with the Same Denominator, Like Fractions		1. Subtract the numerators and place the difference over the original denominator. 2. Reduce the fraction to lowest terms.	Subtract: $\frac{11}{12} - \frac{5}{12}$ $\frac{11-5}{12} = \frac{6}{12} = \frac{1}{2}$
Subtracting Proper Fractions with Different Denominators	13	1. Find the least common denominator. 2. Raise each fraction to the denominator of the LCD. 3. Now, follow the same procedure used to subtract "like" fractions.	Subtract: $\frac{7}{8} - \frac{2}{3}$ $LCD = 8 \times 3 = 24$ $\frac{21}{24} - \frac{16}{24} = \frac{5}{24}$

Subtracting Mixed Numbers	18-22-23	1. If the fractions of the mixed numbers have the same denominator, subtract them and reduce to lowest terms. 2. If the fractions don't have the same denominator, raise them to the denominator of the LCD, and subtract. 3. Subtract the whole numbers. 4. Add the difference of the whole numbers and the difference of the fractions.	Subtract: $15\frac{5}{8} - 12\frac{1}{2}$ $15\frac{5}{8} = 15\frac{5}{8}$ $-12\frac{1}{2} = -12\frac{4}{8}$ $= 3\frac{1}{8}$
Subtracting Mixed Numbers, Using "Borrowing"	22-23	When the numerator of the fraction in the minuend is less than the numerator of the fraction in the subtrahend, we must <u>borrow</u> one "whole" unit from the whole number of the minuend. This will be in the form of the LCD/LCD, and is added to the fraction of the minuend. Now, subtract as before.	Subtract: $6\frac{1}{7} - 2\frac{5}{7}$ $6\frac{1}{7} = 5\frac{7}{7} + \frac{1}{7} = 5\frac{8}{7}$ $-2\frac{5}{7}$ $\qquad -2\frac{5}{7}$ $\qquad = 3\frac{3}{7}$
Multiplication of Fractions	16-17-24-25	1. Multiply all the numerators to form the new numerator. 2. Multiply all the denominators to form the new denominator. 3. If necessary, reduce the answer to lowest terms.	Multiply: $\frac{5}{8} \times \frac{2}{3}$ $\frac{5}{8} \times \frac{2}{3} = \frac{10}{24} = \frac{5}{12}$
Multiplication of Fractions, Using "Cancellation"	17-21-22-24-25	**Cancellation** simplifies the numbers with which we are dealing, and leaves the answer in lowest terms. To apply cancellation, use the following steps: 1. Find a common factor that divides evenly into at least one of the denominators, and one of the numerators. 2. Divide that common factor into the denominator and the numerator, thereby reducing it. 3. Repeat this process until there are no more common factors. 4. Now multiply the fractions, as before. The resulting product will be in lowest terms.	Use cancellation to solve the multiplication problem above: **Cancellation Method:** $\frac{5}{8} \times \frac{2}{3} = \frac{5}{\underset{4}{8}} \times \frac{\overset{1}{2}}{3} = \frac{5}{12}$

Multiplying Mixed Numbers	19-20-21-22-23-25	1. Convert all mixed numbers to improper fractions. 2. Multiply, as before, using cancellation wherever possible. 3. If the answer is an improper fraction, convert it to a whole or mixed number. 4. Reduce to lowest terms. **Note:** When multiplying fractions times whole numbers, change the whole numbers to fractions by placing them over 1.	Multiply: $3\frac{1}{2} \times 2\frac{3}{8}$ $3\frac{1}{2} = \frac{7}{2}$ $2\frac{3}{8} = \frac{19}{8}$ $\frac{7}{2} \times \frac{19}{8} = \frac{133}{16} = 8\frac{5}{16}$
Division of Fractions and Mixed Numbers	15-20	Division of fractions requires that we **invert** the divisor. To invert means to turn upside down. By inverting a fraction, the numerator becomes the denominator, and the denominator becomes the numerator. The inverted fraction is also known as a **reciprocal.** Dividing fractions: 1. Convert all mixed numbers to improper fractions. 2. Identify the fraction that is the divisor, and invert. 3. Change the "divided by" sign, ÷, to a "multiplied by" sign, x. 4. Multiply the fractions. 5. Reduce the answer to lowest terms.	Divide: $\frac{11}{12} \div \frac{2}{3}$ 11/12 is the **dividend** 2/3 is the **divisor** $\frac{11}{12} \div \frac{2}{3} = \frac{11}{12} \times \frac{3}{2}$ $\frac{11}{\overset{12}{\underset{4}{}}} \times \frac{\overset{1}{3}}{2} = \frac{11}{8} = 1\frac{3}{8}$

ASSESSMENT EXERCISE #2
Fractions

For each of the following, identify the type of fraction and write it in word form:

1. $^{18}/_{11}$ **2.** $4\frac{1}{6}$ **3.** $^{13}/_{16}$

Convert to whole or mixed numbers:

4. $^{57}/_9$ **5.** $^{125}/_5$

Convert to improper fractions:

6. $12\frac{3}{4}$ **7.** $9\frac{5}{8}$

Reduce to lowest terms:

8. $^{96}/_{108}$ **9.** $^{26}/_{65}$

Convert to higher terms, as indicated:

10. $^4/_5$ to twenty-fifths   **11.** $^3/_{13}$ to seventy-eighths

Find the least common denominator for the following fractions:

12. $\frac{3}{4}$, $^{19}/_{20}$, $\frac{1}{6}$, $\frac{3}{5}$, $^8/_{15}$

Solve the following problems, and reduce to lowest terms:

13. $3/4 - 1/18$ **14.** $2/3 + 1/6 + 11/12$ **15.** $2/3 \div 1/8$ **16.** $5/6 \times 1/4$

Solve the following word problems:

17. Chuck Bradley earns $161 per day. On Thursday he worked $3/7$ of a day. How much did Chuck earn that day?

18. Maria Lopez worked $6\frac{1}{8}$ hours on Monday, $7\frac{3}{4}$ hours on Tuesday, and $4\frac{1}{2}$ hours on Wednesday. If Maria wants to work 25 hours this week, how many more hours must she work?

19. A union takes $1/25$ of John's wages as dues. If he made $825 last week, how much in dues was deducted?

20. On a canned fruit assembly line, a large container holds 255 gallons of fruit salad.
   A. If each can holds $5/12$ of a gallon, how many cans does the container fill?

   B. If the process uses $2\frac{3}{4}$ containers per hour, how many cans are packed in an 8 hour day?

21. A developer owns 3 lots measuring $1\frac{2}{3}$ acres each, 4 lots of $3\frac{3}{4}$ acres each, and 1 lot measuring $2\frac{3}{8}$ acres.

A. What is the total acreage owned by the developer?

B. If each acre is worth $10,000, what is the total value of the properties?

22. A manufacturer has been using glass jars weighing $11\frac{2}{3}$ ounces each. If the company switched to synthetic jars, weighing $7\frac{5}{6}$ ounces,

A. How many ounces would be saved per 48-jar carton?

B. If there are 16 ounces in a pound, how many pounds would be saved?

23. Louis Chang bought stock for $\$96\frac{3}{4}$ per share, and sold it for $\$113\frac{7}{8}$ per share. If he had 1,000 shares, how much profit did he make?

24. J C Penney advertised "$\frac{1}{4}$ OFF" the list price of Model II microwave ovens, and an additional "$\frac{1}{5}$ OFF" the list price for ovens which are scratched.

A. If the list price of Model II is $240, what is the sale price?

B. What is the price of a scratched one?

25.   Among other ingredients, a recipe for linguini with red sauce calls for the following: 24 ounces of linguini pasta, 5 cups fresh tomatoes, and 8 tablespoons of parmesan cheese. If this recipe serves 8 people, recalculate the quantities to serve 5 people.

Decimals
Summary Chart

Topic	A/E#	Important Concepts	Illustrative Examples
Writing Decimals in Word and Numerical Form	1-2-3-4-5-6-7	In **decimals,** the value of each place, starting at the decimal point and moving from left to right, decreases by a factor of "10." The names of the **"places"** end in *ths;* they are tenths, hundredths, thousandths, ten-thousandths, hundred- thousandths, and millionths. 1. To write **decimal numbers** in words, write the decimal part as if it were a whole number, then name the place value of the last digit on the right. 2. Writing **mixed decimals,** the decimal point should be read as "*and.*" 3. If the decimal has a **fraction** at the end, simply read them together, using the place value of the last digit of the decimal. 4. When a **dollar sign, $,** precedes a number, the whole number value represents dollars, the decimal value represents cents, and the decimal point is read as "and."	0.0691 is, "six hundred ninety-one ten-thousandths." Twenty-one ten-thousandths is ".0021" ———————— 51.305 is, "fifty-one and three hundred five thousandths." Eighteen and thirty-six thousandths is "18.036" ———————— .22½ is, "twenty-two and one-half hundredths." Seventeen and one-half hundredths is ".17½" ———————— $946.73 is , "nine hundred forty-six dollars and seventy-three cents." Six dollars and twelve cents is "6.12"
Rounding Decimal Numbers to a Specified Place Value	8-9-10-11	1. Determine the place to which the decimal is to be rounded. 2a. If the digit to the right of the one being rounded is 5 or more, increase the digit in the place being rounded by 1. 2b. If the digit to the right of the one being rounded is 4 or less, do not change the digit in the place being rounded. 3. Delete all digits to the right of the one being rounded.	.645 rounded to hundredths is ".65" 42.5596 rounded to tenths is "42.6" .00291 rounded to thousandths is ".003" $75.888 rounded to cents is "$75.89"
Addition and Subtraction of Decimals	12-13-14-15-16-17-24-25-26-27-28-29-30	**Addition and subtraction** of decimals requires lining up all the place values, including the decimal points. The decimal point in the answer will appear in the same position (column) as in the problem. When all the numbers have been lined up, you may add zeros to the right of the decimal numbers that do not have enough places.	2821.049 12.500 + 143.008 2976.557 194.1207 –45.3400 148.7807

Multiplication of Decimals	18-19-20-24-26-27-28-29-30	1. Multiply the numbers as if they are whole numbers, disregarding the decimal points. 2. "Total" the number of decimal places in the multiplier and the multiplicand. 3. Insert the decimal point in the product giving it the same number of decimal places as the total from step 2. 4. If necessary, place zeros to the left of the digits in the product to provide the correct number of digits to the right of the decimal point. **Note:** If the situation involves money, answers should be rounded to the nearest cent.	Multiply 224.5 by 4.53 $\quad$ 224.5 $\quad$ 1 decimal place $\times$ 4.53 $\quad$ 2 decimal places $\quad$ 6735 $\quad$ 11225 $\quad$ 8980 1016.985 $\quad$ 3 decimal places
Multiplication Shortcut: Powers of "10"	20-27	Whenever you are multiplying a decimal times a power of 10, such as 10, 100, 1,000, 10,000, etc., 1. Count the number of zeros in the multiplier and move the decimal point in the multiplicand the same number of places to the right. 2. If necessary, add zeros to the product to provide the required places.	$46.339 \times 10 = 463.39$ $\quad$ 1 place $46.339 \times 100 = 4633.9$ $\quad$ 2 places $46.339 \times 1,000 = 46339$ $\quad$ 3 places $46.339 \times 10,000 = 463390$ $\qquad\qquad\qquad\qquad$ 4 places $46.339 \times 100,000 = 4633900$ $\qquad\qquad\qquad\qquad$ 5 places
Division of Decimals	21-22-23-30	<u>If the divisor is a whole number</u> 1. Place the decimal point in the quotient directly above the decimal point in the dividend. 2. Divide the numbers. <u>If the divisor is a decimal number</u> 1. Move the decimal point in the divisor to the right until it becomes a whole number. 2. Move the decimal point in the dividend the same number of places as that of the divisor. It may be necessary to add zeros to the right of the dividend if there are not enough places. 3. Place the decimal point in the quotient directly above the decimal point in the dividend. 4. Divide the numbers $\quad$ **Note:** All answers involving money should be rounded to the nearest cent. This means dividing until the quotient has a thousandths place, and then rounding back to hundredths.	Divide: $9.5 \div 25$ $\quad\quad$ .38 $25\overline{)9.50}$ $\quad\quad$ 75 $\quad\quad$ 200 $\quad\quad$ 200 $\quad\quad\quad$ 0 Divide: $14.3 \div 2.2$ $2.2\overline{)14.3}$ $\quad\quad$ 6.5 $22\overline{)143.0}$ $\quad\quad$ 132 $\quad\quad$ 110 $\quad\quad$ 110 $\quad\quad\quad$ 0

Division Shortcut "Powers of 10"	22	Whenever you divide a decimal by a "power of 10," such as 10, 100, 1,000, 10,000, etc., 1. Count the number of zeros in the divisor, and move the decimal point in the dividend the same number of places to the left. 2. It may be necessary to add zeros to provide the required number of decimal places.	$21.69 \div 10 = 2.169$ 1 place $21.69 \div 100 = .2169$ 2 places $21.69 \div 1,000 = .02169$ 3 places $21.69 \div 10,000 = .002169$ 4 places
Converting Decimals to Fractions		1. Write the decimal as a fraction by making the decimal number, without the decimal point, the numerator. 2. The denominator is "1" followed by as many zeros as there are decimal places in the original decimal number. 3. Reduce the fraction to lowest terms.	$.88 = 88/100 = 22/25$ $5.57 = 5 + {}^{57}/_{100} = 5{}^{57}/_{100}$
Converting Fractions to Decimals		1. Divide the numerator by the denominator. 2. Add a decimal point and zeros, as necessary, to the numerator.	$4/5 = 5\overline{)4.0}^{.8}$ $22/4 = 4\overline{)22.0}^{5.5}$

ASSESSMENT EXERCISE #3
Decimals

Write the following decimal numbers in word form:

1. 0.0602   **2.** 34.481   **3.** $119.85

Write the following decimal numbers in numerical form:

4. Nine hundred sixty-seven ten-thousandths

5. Five and fourteen thousandths

6. Six thousand, eight hundred forty-three and fifteen hundredths

7. Sixteen dollars and fifty-seven cents

Round the following numbers to the indicated place:

8. 0.44857 to hundredths   **9.** 995.06966 to tenths

10. $127.94 to dollars   **11.** $4.2480 to dollars and cents

Perform the indicated operation for the following:

12. 6.003 + 45.068

13. $1.58 + $15.63 + $19.81 + $.17

14. .003 + 69.271 +193.55 + 211

15. 23.0556 – 15.35

16. $95.67 – $2.84

17. 0.903 – 0.066

18. 14.74
$\times$ 15

19.   6.5
$\times$ .024

20. 0.9912 $\times$ 100,000

21. 8.65 $\div$ .5

22. 790.4 $\div$ 10,000

23. $150.45 $\div$ 7.5

Using a calculator, solve the following word problems:

24.   Paul Clinton went shopping for a stereo. He purchased an AM-FM tuner for $335.79, a control amplifier for $435.67, and a CD player for $287.99. He also bought 2 CDs for $11.88 each and 3 CDs for $14.88 each. What was the total amount of Paul's purchase?

25. Mike's Bikes has a 22" off-road racer on sale this month for $239.95. If the original price of the bike was $315.10, how much will a customer save by purchasing a bike during the sale?

26. Joe and Gloria both work for the Lisette Company. Joe earns $17.75 per hour as a technician, Gloria earns $19.50 per hour as a research analyst. Last week Joe worked 43.22 hours and Gloria worked 37.6 hours. What was their total earnings for the week? Round to the nearest cent.

27. Great Impressions, a printing company, charges $.066 per page for color brochures.
   A. What is the cost of 10,000 copies of a 4-page brochure?

   B. If PayLess Printers will do the job for $.061, how much can be saved by using them to print the brochure?

28. Harry Morgan owes the Mountain City Bank $34,880.41. If he makes monthly payments of $546.11 for 2 years, what is the balance remaining on Harry's loan?

29. The Academy Lumber Company wants to deliver 145 sheets of plywood, each weighing 18.6 pounds, and 64 bags of concrete mix, each weighing 69.7 pounds. If Academy's small delivery truck has a capacity of 6,500 pounds, can this order be shipped in one truckload?

30.   Keith Wallach wanted to make some money at a flea market. He purchased 55 small plants from a nursery for a total of $137.80, 3 bags of potting soil for $2.65 each, and 55 ceramic pots at $4.60 each. At the next flea market, Keith sold all 55 plants for $15.00 each.

A.   What was his total cost per plant?

B.   How much total profit did Keith make on this venture?

Student Notes

Section I
Assessment Test

(Use the Answer Sheet provided at the end of this test.)

1. Alan Williamson had $1,244 in his checking account on November 1. During the month he wrote checks for $34, $23, $177, $436, and $69. He also deposited $133, $54, and $87. What is the balance in Alan's checking account at the end of November?

2. Lynn Highland bought a 16-acre piece of property for $27,648.
   A. What was the price per acre?

   B. If the taxes amount to $125 per acre, what are the total taxes due on the property?

3. Bernard White earned $387 last week. If he worked 43 hours, what is his hourly rate of pay?

4. Bill Ding, a project manager, estimated that a construction job would take 71½ hours to complete.
   A. If workers spent 12½ hours Monday, 14¼ hours Tuesday, 13¾ hours Wednesday, and 18¼ hours Thursday, how many hours will be needed on Friday to complete the project?

   B. If workers earn $9.80 per hour, and the cost of materials is $2,500, what is the total cost of the project?

5. A college has 3,600 students. In-state students pay $550 tuition per semester, and out-of-state students pay $795. If ⅝ of the students are from out-of-state, how much revenue does the college take in per semester?

6. Lorna Strickland bought 750 shares of stock at $25⅛ per share. When the stock hit $46¾ she sold the shares. How much profit did Lorna make?

7. The Bamster Coal Mining Company can produce 460 tons of ore in an 8-hour shift. The mine operates continuously, 3 shifts per day, 7 days per week. How many tons of coal can be mined in a 30-day month?

8. Fancy Fruit Wholesalers purchased 351 crates of apples from the Sun-Ripe Orchard. They intend to repack the apples in smaller boxes to be shipped to supermarkets. If each box contains ⅜ of a crate, how many boxes can be packed?

9. A carpenter spent $18.85 on nails. If nails sell for $.65 per pound, how many pounds did the carpenter purchase?

10. You are the payroll manager for the Rand Company. Rounding to dollars and cents, complete the following payroll data sheet:

EMPLOYEE	HOURS	HOURLY WAGE	TOTAL	DEDUCTIONS	NET PAY
Williams	37.6	$6.80	_____	$51.68	_____
Johnson	43.22	$8.25	_____	$102.64	_____
Calder	39.37	$10.47	_____	_____	$287.95
Sanford	27.7	_____	$487.52	$122.63	_____

11.   A clothing manufacturer buys material in large rolls containing 456 yards each. Pants require 2¾ yards of material, vests ⅞ of a yard, and jackets 3½ yards.
A. How many yards of material are required to make one suit?

B. How many complete 3-piece suits can be made from each roll?

12.   **A.** What is the cost of 2,000 shares of stock selling at $9⅜ per share?

B. If the broker's commission is $458.23, what is the total cost of the transaction?

13.   A soft drink vending truck has a tank that holds 460 quarts of soda. Last Saturday, at a carnival, the owner sold out completely. He sells a 10-ounce drink for $1.25. There are 16 ounces in a pint, and 2 pints in a quart.
A. How many drinks did he serve?

B. How much money did he take in for the day?

14.   Fran and Honey own a catering business. They have a recipe for noodle pudding that serves four people. If they want to make the pudding for a dinner party, serving ten people, calculate the new amount for each ingredient.

Ingredient	Quantity (4 people)	Quantity (10 people)
cooked noodles	24 ounces	_____
sour cream	2 4/5 cups	_____
sugar	2/3 cup	_____
cinnamon	1 1/3 tablespoons	_____
pitted cherries	7 1/2 ounces	_____
vanilla	3/4 teaspoon	_____
eggs	2 eggs	_____

15.   A shopping center owner received $358,925 in rent from tenants last month. If the center charges rent of $2.45 per square foot,

   A. How many square feet are in the shopping center?

   B. If maintenance costs are $.024 per square foot, per month, what is the total cost of maintenance per month?

BUSINESS DECISION:
"Al's Custom Tailor Shop"

16.   Al Weinberger, a custom tailor, buys fabric in rolls containing 171 yards each. Pants require 2 3/4 yards of material, vests require 7/8 of a yard, and jackets take 3 1/2 yards.

A. How many yards of material are required for each complete suit?

B. How many suits can Al make from each roll?

C. If each roll of 100% wool material costs $1,800, what is the cost of material per suit?

D. If Al adds labor and overhead charges of $290 per suit, and profit of $100 per suit, how much should he charge for a custom-made suit?

Course _____   Name _____
Term: _____   St# _____
Professor _____   Date: _____

A Little Math With Your Business
Assessment Test - Section I

Answer Sheet

1. _____   5. _____
2A _____   6. _____
2B. _____   7. _____
3. _____   8. _____
4A. _____   9. _____
4B. _____

10.

EMPLOYEE	HOURS	HOURLY WAGE	TOTAL	DEDUCTIONS	NET PAY
Williams	37.6	$ 6.80	$_____	$ 51.68	$_____
Johnson	43.22	$ 8.25	$_____	$102.64	$_____
Calder	39.37	$10.47	$_____	$_____	$287.95
Sanford	27.7	$_____	$487.52	$122.63	$_____

11A. _____   15A. _____
11B. _____   15B. _____
12A. _____   16A. _____
12B. _____   16B. _____
13A. _____   16C. _____
13B. _____   16D. _____

14.   cooked noodles   _____
      sour cream   _____
      sugar   _____
      cinnamon   _____
      pitted cherries   _____
      vanilla   _____
      eggs   _____

Section II

Percents
and Their
Application in Business

SECTION II

PERCENTS AND THEIR APPLICATION IN BUSINESS

PART I   UNDERSTANDING AND CONVERTING PERCENTS

It takes only a glance at the business section of a newspaper, or an annual report of a company, to see how extensively percents are applied in business. Percents are the primary way of measuring change among business variables. For example, "Revenue is up 6% this year," or "Expenses have been cut by 2.3% this month." Interest rates, commissions, and many taxes are expressed in percent form. "Sunnyside Bank charged 12 percent on the loan," "A real estate broker made 5% commission on the sale of the property," or "The state charges a 6½% sales tax." Even price changes are frequently advertised as percents, "Sears Dishwasher Sale—All Models, 25% Off!"

To this point, we have learned that fractions and decimals are two ways of representing parts of a "whole thing." Percents are another way of expressing quantity with relation to a whole.

Percent means "per hundred," or "parts per hundred," and is represented by the percent sign, %. Percents are numbers equal to a fraction with a denominator of 100. "Five percent," for example, means 5 parts out of 100, and may be written in the following ways:

$$5 \text{ percent} \quad 5\% \quad 5 \text{ hundredths} \quad 5/100 \quad .05$$

Before we can perform any mathematical calculations with percents, they must be converted to either decimals or fractions. Part I of this section covers the procedures for making these conversions. Parts II and III introduce some very important applications of percents in business.

Converting Percents to Decimals and Decimals to Percents

Since percents are numbers expressed as parts per 100, the percent sign, %, means multiplication by $\frac{1}{100}$. Therefore:

$$25\% = 25 \times \frac{1}{100} = 25/100 = .25$$

---

1. Converting a percent to a decimal

Steps for <u>converting a percent to a decimal</u>:

1. Remove the percent sign.
2. Move the decimal point two places to the left.
   Remember, if there is no decimal point, it is understood to be to the right of the digit in the ones place, [2 = 2.].
3. If the percent is a fraction, such as $\frac{4}{5}\%$, or a mixed number, such as $9\frac{1}{2}\%$, first change the fraction part to a decimal, then follow steps 1 and 2 above. For example:
   $$\frac{3}{8}\% = .375\% \qquad 4\frac{3}{4}\% = 4.75\%$$

EXAMPLE 1

Convert each of the following percents to decimals:

A. 44%   **B.** 233%   **C.** 56.4%   **D.** .68%   **E.** 18¼%   **F.** ⅛%

SOLUTION STRATEGY_____

Following the steps for converting percents to decimals, we move the decimal point two places to the left, and remove the percent sign:

A. 44% = .44   **B.** 233% = 2.33   **C.** 56.4% = .564

D. .68% = .0068   **E.** 18¼% = 18.25% = .1825   **F.** ⅛% = .125% = .00125

TRY-IT EXERCISES

Convert each of the following percents to decimals:

1. 27%   **2.** 472%   **3.** 93.7%   **4.** .81%   **5.** 12¾%   **6.** ⅞%

Check your answers with the correct answers and worked-out solutions in the appendix.

---

2. Converting a decimal or whole number to a percent

Steps for <u>converting decimals and whole numbers to percents</u>:

1. Move the decimal point two places to the right.

2. Add a percent sign to the number.

3. Once again, if there are fractions involved, convert them to decimals first, then proceed with steps 1 and 2 above. For example:

$$.02\tfrac{3}{4} = .0275 = 2.75\%$$

EXAMPLE 2

Convert each of the following decimals or whole numbers to percents:

A. .5   **B.** 3.7   **C.** .044   **D.** .09⅗   **E.** 7   **F.** .6½

SOLUTION STRATEGY_____

Following the steps for converting decimals to percents, we move the decimal point two places to the right, and add the percent sign.

A. .5 = 50%   **B.** 3.7 = 370%   **C.** .044 = 4.4%

D. .09⅗ = .096 = 9.6%   **E.** 7 = 700%   **F.** .6½ = .65 = 65%

| **TRY-IT EXERCISES** |

Convert each of the following decimals or whole numbers to percents:

7. .8   **8.** 1.4   **9.** .0023   **10.** .016⅔   **11.** 19   **12.** .57⅔

Check your answers with the correct answers and worked-out solutions in the appendix.

PART II   USING THE PERCENTAGE FORMULA TO SOLVE BUSINESS PROBLEMS

Now that we have learned to convert percents, let's take a look at some practical applications in business. Percent problems involve the use of three equations known as the "percentage formulas." These have three variables: the **base,** the **percentage** or **portion,** and the **rate.** In business situations, two of the variables will be given, and are the **knowns,** while one of the variables will be the **unknown.**

Once the variables have been properly identified, the equations are quite simple to solve. The variables have the following characteristics, which should be used to help identify them:

Base: The base is the number that represents 100%, or the **"whole thing."** It is the starting point or total value of something. The base is often preceded by the word "of" in the written statement of the situation.

Percentage: The percentage is the number that represents a **"part"** or **"portion"** of the base. The percentage is always in the "same terms" as the base. For example, if the base is dollars, the percentage is dollars; if the base is people, the percentage is people; if the base is production units, so is the percentage.

Note: the percentage is **NOT** the number with the percent, %, sign.
The percentage often has a unique characteristic that is being measured or compared to the base. For example, the base might be the total number of cars produced, and the percentage would be the "portion" of the total cars that are 4-door sedans (the unique characteristic).

Rate: The rate is easily identified. It is the variable with the **%** sign, or the word percent. It defines "how much," expressed in percent, the percentage is of the base. If the rate is under 100%, the percentage is less than the base; if the rate is 100%, the percentage is equal to the base; and if the rate is over 100%, the percentage is greater than the base.

The following formulas are used to solve percent problems:

$$\text{Percentage} = \text{Rate} \times \text{Base} \qquad\qquad \mathbf{P = R \times B}$$

$$\text{Rate} = \frac{\text{Percentage}}{\text{Base}} \qquad\qquad R = \frac{P}{B}$$

$$\text{Base} = \frac{\text{Percentage}}{\text{Rate}} \qquad\qquad B = \frac{P}{R}$$

Steps for solving percentage equations:

> 1. Identify the two knowns and the unknown.
> 2. Choose the formula that solves for the unknown.
> 3. Solve the equation by substituting the known values for the letters in the formula.

An easy method for remembering the percentage formulas is by using the Magic Pyramid!!

THE MAGIC PYRAMID

The pyramid is divided into 3 sections, representing the percentage, rate, and base. By circling or covering the letter in the pyramid that corresponds to the unknown of the problem, the pyramid will "magically" reveal the correct formula to use.

P = R x B

PERCENTAGE

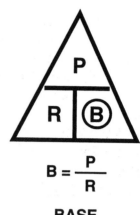

$$R = \frac{P}{B}$$

RATE

$$B = \frac{P}{R}$$

BASE

3. Solving for the percentage

P = R x B

Remember, the percentage is a "part" or "portion" of the whole, and will always be in the same terms as the base. It is found by multiplying the rate times the base (P = R × B). The following examples will demonstrate solving for the percentage:

| EXAMPLE 3 |

What is the percentage, if the base is $400, and the rate is 12%?

SOLUTION STRATEGY_____

In this basic problem, we simply substitute the known numbers for the letters in the formula, percentage = rate × base. In this problem, 12% is the **rate,** and $400 is the **base.** Don't forget to convert the percent (rate) to a decimal by deleting the % sign and moving the decimal point two places to the left (12% = .12).

$P = R \times B$
$P = 12\% \times 400$
$P = .12 \times 400$
$P = 48$
Percentage = $48

| EXAMPLE 4 |

What number is 43.5% of 250?

SOLUTION STRATEGY

In this problem, the **rate** is easily identified as the term with the % sign. The **base,** or whole amount, is preceded by the word "of." We use the formula percentage = rate × base, substituting the knowns for the letters that represent them.

$P = R \times B$
$P = 43.5\% \times 250$
$P = .435 \times 250$
$P = 108.75$
Percentage = 108.75

EXAMPLE 5

An electronics firm makes 6,000 radios per day. If 2% of them are defective, how many defective radios are produced each day?

SOLUTION STRATEGY

To solve this problem, we must first identify the variables. Since 2% has the percent sign, it is the **rate.** The terms are radios, the total, 6,000, is the **base.** The unique characteristic of the **percentage,** the unknown, is that they are defective. Again, we use the percentage formula:

$P = R \times B$
$P = .02 \times 6,000$
$P = 120$
Percentage = 120 defective units per day

TRY-IT EXERCISES

Solve each of the following for the percentage:

13. What is the percentage if the base is 980 and the rate is 55%?

14. What number is 75% of 3,220?

15. A company has 1,250 employees, of which 16% constitute the sales staff. How many employees are in sales?

16. If Sunshine Savings & Loan requires a 15% down payment on a mortgage loan, what is the down payment needed to finance a $148,500 home?

Check your answers with the correct answers and worked-out solutions in the appendix.

4. Solving for the rate

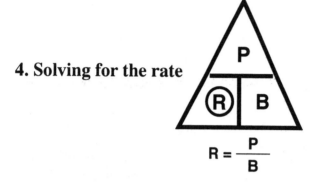

$$R = \frac{P}{B}$$

The rate is the variable that describes what "portion" or "part" of the base is represented by the percentage. It is <u>always</u> the term with the percent sign. When solving for the rate, your answer will be a decimal. Be sure to convert the decimal to a percent, by moving the decimal point two places to the right and adding a percent sign. We use the formula rate = percentage ÷ base, $R = P \div B$. The following examples demonstrate solving for the rate:

EXAMPLE 6

What is the rate if the base is 160 and the percentage is 40?

SOLUTION STRATEGY_____

In this basic problem, we simply substitute the known numbers for the letters in the formula, rate = percentage ÷ base.

$$R = \frac{P}{B}$$

$$R = \frac{40}{160}$$

$$R = .25 = 25\%$$

<u>Rate = 25%</u>

EXAMPLE 7

What percent of 700 is 56?

SOLUTION STRATEGY_____

This problem asks, "what percent," indicating that the **rate** is the unknown. The 700 is preceded by the word "of," and is therefore the **base.** The 56 is part of the base, and is therefore the **percentage.** Once again we use the formula: rate = percentage ÷ base, substituting the knowns for the letters that represent them.

$$R = \frac{P}{B}$$

$$R = \frac{56}{700}$$

$$R = .08 = 8\%$$

$$\underline{Rate = 8\%}$$

EXAMPLE 8

A retail chain of pet shops placed an order for 560 fish tanks. If only 490 tanks were delivered, what percent of the order was received?

SOLUTION STRATEGY_____

The first step in solving this problem is to identify the variables. The statement asks, "what percent," consequently the **rate** is the unknown. Since 560 is the "total" order, it is the **base.** Because 490 is a "part" of the total, it is the **percentage.** Note that the base and the percentage are in the same terms, fish tanks. The "unique characteristic" of the percentage is that the 490 tanks <u>were</u> delivered. Once again, we use the rate formula:

$$R = \frac{P}{B}$$

$$R = \frac{490}{560}$$

$$R = .875 = 87.5\%$$

$$\underline{Rate = 87.5\%}$$

TRY-IT EXERCISES

Solve each of the following for the rate, rounding to tenths when necessary.

17. What is the rate if the base is 22 and the percentage is 9?

18. 67 is what percent of 142?

19. A contract called for 18,000 square feet of tile to be installed in a shopping mall. In the first week 5,400 square feet was completed. What percent of the job has been completed?

20. During a recent sale, Image Makers, a boutique shop, sold $5,600 in men's business suits. If total sales amounted to $8,970, what percent of the sales were suits?

Check your answers with the correct answers and worked-out solutions in the appendix.

5. Solving for the base

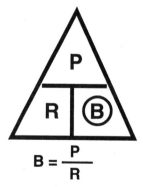

In order to solve business situations in which the "whole" or "total amount" is the unknown, we use the formula base = percentage ÷ rate, $B = \dfrac{P}{R}$.

The following examples illustrate solving for the base:

EXAMPLE 9

What is the base if the rate is 21% and the percentage is 58.8?

SOLUTION STRATEGY_____

In this basic problem, we simply substitute the known values for the letters in the formula. Remember, the rate must be converted from a percent to a decimal.

$$B = \frac{P}{R}$$

$$B = \frac{58.8}{21\%}$$

$$B = \frac{58.8}{.21}$$

$$B = 280$$

Base = 280

EXAMPLE 10

792 is 15% of what number?

SOLUTION STRATEGY_____

Remember, the **base** is usually identified as the value preceded by "of" in the statement. In this case, that value is the unknown. Because it has the percent sign, 15 is the **rate;** 792 is the "part" of the whole, or the **percentage.**

$$B = \frac{P}{R}$$

$$B = \frac{792}{15\%}$$

$$B = \frac{792}{.15}$$

$$B = 5,280$$

Base = 5,280

EXAMPLE 11

Sidekicks, an athletic shoe store chain, reports that 28% of total sales are from Nike shoes and other Nike products. If last week's Nike sales were $15,640.80, what is the total amount of sales for the week?

SOLUTION STRATEGY

In this problem, the "total amount" of sales, the **base,** is the unknown. Because it has the percent sign, 28 is the **rate,** and $15,640.80 is the **percentage.** Note again, the percentage is in the same terms as the base, dollar sales. The "unique characteristic" is that the percentage represents <u>Nike</u> sales.

$$B = \frac{P}{R}$$

$$B = \frac{15,640.80}{28\%}$$

$$B = \frac{15,640.80}{.28}$$

$$B = 55,860$$

<u>Base = $55,860</u>

TRY-IT EXERCISES

Solve each of the following for the base:

21. What is the base if the rate is 40% and the percentage is 690?

22. $545.60 is 88% of what amount?

23. In a machine shop, 75% of the motor repairs are for broken shafts. If 120 motors had broken shafts, how many motors were repaired?

24. At Office Depot, 85% of the copy paper sold is letter size. If 3,400 reams of letter size were sold, how many total reams of copy paper were sold?

Check your answers with the correct answers and worked-out solutions in the appendix.

PART III   SOLVING OTHER BUSINESS PROBLEMS INVOLVING PERCENTS

In addition to the basic percentage formula, percents are used in many other ways in business. Measuring increases and decreases, comparing results from one year to another, and reporting economic activity and trends are just a few of these applications.

Fundamental to success in business is the ability of managers to make correct decisions. These decisions require accurate and up-to-date information, and measuring percent changes in business activity is an important source of this information. Percents often describe a situation in a more "informative way" than numbers alone.

For example, a company reports a profit of $50,000 for the year. Although the number $50,000 is correct, it doesn't give a "perspective" of whether that amount of profit is good or bad. A comparison to last years figures, using percents, might reveal that "profits are up 45% over last year," or "profits are down 66.8%." Significant news!

6. Determining rate of increase or decrease $+\%$ $-\%$

In calculating the rate of increase or decrease of something, we use the same percentage formula concepts as before. Rate of change means "percent" change; therefore, the *rate* is the unknown. We will use the formula $R = P \div B$.

Rate of change situations contain an "original" value or amount of something, which either increases or decreases to a "new" value or amount.

In solving these problems, the "original" value is always the **base,** and the difference between the original and the "new" is the **percentage.** The unknown is the **rate,** which describes the percent change between the two amounts.

Steps for calculating rate of increase or decrease:

> 1. Identify the "original" and the "new" amounts, and find the difference between them.
> 2. Using the rate formula, $R = P \div B$, substitute the difference from step 1 above for the percentage, and the original amount for the base.
> 3. Solve the equation for R. Remember, your answer will be in decimal form, which must be converted to a percent.

The following examples illustrate how we perform this procedure:

EXAMPLE 12

If a number increases from 60 to 75, what is the rate of increase?

SOLUTION STRATEGY

In this basic problem, a number changes from 60 to 75, and we are looking for the percent change—in this case an increase. The original amount is 60, the new amount is 75.

Using the steps above, the percentage is the difference between the amounts, $75 - 60 = 15$, and the base is the original amount, 60. We now substitute these values into the formula:

$$R = \frac{P}{B}$$

$$R = \frac{15}{60}$$

$$R = .25 = 25\%$$

<u>Rate of increase = 25%</u>

EXAMPLE 13

A number decreased from 120 to 80. What is the percent decrease?

SOLUTION STRATEGY

This problem illustrates a number decreasing in value. The unknown is the **rate** of decrease. From the steps above, we identify the original amount as 120, and the new amount as 80.

The difference between them is the **percentage,** $120 - 80 = 40$. The original amount, 120, is the **base.** We now apply the formula:

$$R = \frac{P}{B}$$

$$R = \frac{40}{120}$$

$$R = .333 = 33.3\%$$

Rate of decrease = 33.3%

EXAMPLE 14

Last year a company had a work force of 360 employees. This year there are 510 employees. What is the rate of change in the number of employees? Round your answer to hundredths.

SOLUTION STRATEGY_____

The key to solving this problem is to properly identify the variables. The problem asks, "what is the rate"; therefore, the **rate** is the unknown. The original amount, 360 employees, is the **base.** The difference between the two amounts, 510 – 360 = 150, is the **percentage.** We now apply the rate formula:

$$R = \frac{P}{B}$$

$$R = \frac{150}{360}$$

$$R = .41666 = 41.67\%$$

Rate of increase in employees = 41.67%

EXAMPLE 15

A retail store had revenue of $122,300 in May, and $104,920 in June. What is the percent change in revenue from May to June? Round your answer to the nearest tenth percent.

SOLUTION STRATEGY_____

In this problem, the **rate** of change, the unknown, is a decrease. The original amount, $122,300, is the **base.** The difference between the two amounts, $122,300 – $104,920 = $17,380, is the **percentage.** We apply the rate formula:

$$R = \frac{P}{B}$$

$$R = \frac{17,380}{122,300}$$

$$R = .1421 = 14.2\%$$

Rate of decrease in revenue = 14.2%

TRY-IT EXERCISES

Solve the following problems for the rate of increase or decrease. Round to the nearest tenth percent.

25. If a number increases from 650 to 948, what is the rate of increase?

26. If a number decreases from 21 to 15, what is the rate of decrease?

27. When Leonard Ray was promoted from supervisor to manager, he received a salary increase from $450 to $530 per week. What was the percent change in his salary?

28. You are the production manager for the Emory Corporation. After you started a quality control program on the production line, defects per day dropped from 55 to 12. Top management was very pleased with your results, but wanted to know, "What percent decrease does this represent?"

Check your answers with the correct answers and worked-out solutions in the appendix.

7. Determining "amounts" in increase or decrease situations

Finding the "new amount," after a percent change:

Sometimes the "original amount" of something and the rate of change will be known, and the "new amount," after the change, will be the unknown. For example, if a store sold $5,000 in merchandise on Tuesday, and 8% more on Wednesday, what are Wednesday's sales?

Keep in mind that the original amount, or starting point, is always the **base,** and represents 100%. Because the new amount is the total of the original amount, 100%, and the amount of increase, 8%, the **rate** of the new amount is 108% (100% + 8%). If the rate of change had been a decrease instead of an increase, the **rate** would have been 8% less than the base, or 92% (100% - 8%).

The unknown in this situation, the new amount, is the **percentage;** therefore, we use the percentage formula, percentage = rate × base.

Steps for determining "new amount" after a percent change:

> 1. Substitute the "original amount," or starting point, for the **base.**
> 2a. If the rate of change is an increase, add that rate to 100%, to determine the **rate.**
> 2b. If the rate of change is a decrease, subtract that rate from 100%, to determine the **rate.**

The following examples illustrate how these problems are solved:

EXAMPLE 16

An insurance company estimates that the number of claims on homeowner's insurance will increase by 15%. If last year there were 1,240 claims, how many can be expected this year?

SOLUTION STRATEGY_____

Using the percentage formula and the steps above:

Last year's claims, the original amount, is the **base.** Since the rate of change is an increase, we find the **rate** by adding that change to 100%, 100% + 15% = 115%.

$P = R \times B$
$P = 115\% \times 1,240$
$P = 1.15 \times 1,240$
$P = 1,426$
<u>Percentage = 1,426 = number of homeowner's claims expected this year</u>

EXAMPLE 17

A drive-in restaurant sold 25% fewer milk shakes this week than last week. If they sold 380 shakes last week, how many did they sell this week?

SOLUTION STRATEGY_____

Because this situation represents a percent decrease, the **rate** is determined by subtracting the rate of decrease from 100% (100% − 25% = 75%). As usual, the **base** is the original amount.

$$P = R \times B$$
$$P = 75\% \times 380$$
$$P = .75 \times 380$$
$$P = 285$$
$$\underline{Percentage = 285 = \text{number of milk shakes sold this week}}$$

TRY-IT EXERCISES

Solve each of the following business problems for the new amount, after a percent change:

29. A small company has a computer with a 160 megabyte hard drive. If they replace it with a new model containing 30% more capacity, what would be the megabyte capacity of the new hard drive?

30. A delivery truck covers 20% less miles per week during the winter snow season. If the truck averages 650 miles per week during the summer, how many miles can be expected per week during the winter?

Check your answers with the correct answers and worked-out solutions in the appendix.

Finding the "original amount" before a percent change:

In another business problem involving percent change, the new amount is known and the original amount, the **base,** is unknown. For example, a car dealer sold 42 cars today. If this represents a 20% increase from yesterday, how many cars were sold yesterday?

Solving for the original amount is a base problem; therefore we use the formula:
base = percentage ÷ rate.

Steps for calculating "original amount":

> **1.** Substitute the "new amount" for the **percentage.**
> **2a.** If the rate of change is an increase, add that rate to 100% to determine the **rate.**
> **2b.** If the rate of change is a decrease, subtract that rate from 100% to determine the **rate.**

The following examples illustrate how these problems are solved:

EXAMPLE 18

A company found that after an advertising campaign, business in April increased 12% over March. If April sales were $53,760, what were the sales in March?

SOLUTION STRATEGY

Using the formula for the base, and the steps above:

April's sales, the new amount, is the **percentage.** Since the rate of change is an increase, we find the **rate** by adding that change to 100% (100% + 12% = 112%).

$$B = \frac{P}{R}$$

$$B = \frac{53,760}{112\%}$$

$$B = \frac{53,760}{1.12}$$

$$B = 48,000$$

Base = $48,000 = March sales

EXAMPLE 19

The price of a VCR dropped by 15%, to $425. What was the original price?

SOLUTION STRATEGY

Because this problem represents a percent decrease, the **rate** is determined by subtracting the rate of decrease from 100% (100% − 15% = 85%). The **percentage** is the new amount, $425. The "original price," the **base,** is the unknown. Using the formula for the base,

$$B = \frac{P}{R}$$

$$B = \frac{425}{85\%}$$

$$B = \frac{425}{.85}$$

$$B = 500$$

Base = $500 = original price of VCR

Solve the following business situations for the original amount, before a percent change:

31. A harvester can cover 80 acres per day with a new direct-drive system. If this represents an increase of 20% over the conventional chain-drive system, how many acres per day were covered with the old chain-drive? Round to the nearest tenth.

32. The water level in a large holding tank decreased to 12 feet. If it is down 40% from last week, what was last week's level?

Check your answers with the correct answers and worked-out solutions in the appendix.

8. Understanding and solving problems involving percentage points

Percentage points are another way of expressing a change from an original amount to a new amount, without using the percent sign. When percentage points are used, it is assumed that the base amount, 100%, stays constant. For example, if a company's market share increased from 40 to 44 percent of a total market, this is expressed as, "an increase of 4 percentage points."

The actual percent change in business, however, is calculated using the formula:

$$\text{Rate of change} = \frac{\textbf{change in percentage points}}{\textbf{original amount of percentage points}}$$

In this illustration, the change in percentage points is 4, and the original amount of percentage points is 40. Therefore,

$$\text{Rate of change} = \frac{4}{40} = .10 = 10\% = \text{percent increase in business}$$

EXAMPLE 20

When a competitor built a better mouse trap, a company's market share dropped from 56 to 45 percent of the total market, a drop of 11 percentage points. What percent decrease in business did this represent? Round to the nearest tenth percent.

SOLUTION STRATEGY_____

In this problem, the change in percentage points is 11, and the original market share is 56. Using the formula to find rate of change:

$$\text{Rate of change} = \frac{\text{change in percentage points}}{\text{original amount of percentage points}}$$

$$\text{Rate of change} = \frac{11}{56}$$

$$\text{Rate of change} = .1964 = \underline{19.6\% \text{ decrease in market share}}$$

TRY-IT EXERCISE

33. Prior to an election, a political research firm announced that a candidate for mayor had gained 8 percentage points in the polls this month, from 20 to 28 percent of the total registered voters. What is the candidate's actual percent increase in voters?

Check your answer with the correct answers and worked-out solutions in the appendix.

Student Notes

Section II
Assessment Test
(Use the Answer Sheet provided at the end of this test.)

Solve the following, rounding decimals to hundredths, and percents to tenths:

1. 57% of 1,500 =   **2.** 41.36% of 2.8 =   **3.** 6½% of 46 =

4. What number is 48% of 633?   **5.** What number is 140% of 9?

6. What percent of 75 is 30?   **7.** $128.90 is what percent of $335.65?

8. 45 is _____% of 500   **9.** 388.7 is _____% of 338

10. 86 is 43% of _____   **11.** 459 is 216% of _____   **12.** 5.55 is 18½% of _____

13. If a number increases from 33 to 76, what is the rate of increase?

14. What is the rate of change if the price of an item decreases from $54.60 to $40.95?

15. 560 decreased by 43.5% = _____   **16.** 800 increased by 540% = _____

Solve the following word problems for the unknown, rounding decimals to hundredths, and percents to tenths:

17.   Last season a football team won 12 and lost 8 games. What percent of the games did they win?

18.   Eric Magnum earned $33,500 per year. If he got a 5% raise, what is his new salary?

19.   The price of a refrigerator went from $660 to $495. What is the rate of decrease?

20.   In a recent survey, 306 people preferred instant ice tea over fresh brewed. If that represented 18% of the total respondents, how many people were interviewed?

21.   The Ronson Corporation employs 860 people in three regions of the country. If 30% are in the Midwest region, and 50% in the Northeast region, how many people are employed in the Southern region?

22.   If the sales tax on a purchase of $4,699.03 amounts to $387.67, what is the tax rate?

23. A toy manufacturer gets 34% of its revenue from doll houses. If doll house sales last year were $565,700, what were the total sales of the company?

24. What is the rate of change if the temperature in an oven rises from 188.6 degrees to 375 degrees?

25. A business is owned by three partners, as follows: Ethel owns 27%, Goldie owns 33%, and Fred owns the rest. If Fred's share amounts to $45,000, what is the dollar amount of Ethel's and Goldie's share?

26. Jan Roberts sells appliances for Apple Distributors. Last week she earned $975 in commissions. If her commission rate is 15%, what was the total amount of Jan's sales?

27. A trade show had 564 exhibitors last year, and 768 this year. What is the percent increase in exhibitors?

28. A plant nursery sold $790 in fertilizer in August. If September sales were 18% less, how much fertilizer was sold in September?

29. Ivan is paid a gross salary each week of $565.00. After deductions for taxes, social security, and medical insurance, he receives a check for $440.70.

   A. What percent of his income is taken out for deductions?

   B. If Ivan got a raise to $35,000 per year, based on the same percent of deductions, what would be his new weekly take-home pay?

30. Gel toothpaste had a 32% share of the market last year, and a 37% share this year. If this represents an increase of 5 percentage points, what is the percent increase in Gel toothpaste business?

31. A company depreciates its trucks and equipment for 5 years, and then sells them to used equipment dealers.

   A. If the company paid $8,900 for a forklift 5 years ago, and sold it for $1,780 last week, what percent of the original price was lost to depreciation?

   B. Using the same rate of depreciation as with the forklift, if a conveyor belt transport system was sold after 5 years to a dealer for $1,860, what was the original purchase price of this equipment?

32. Ocean City has a population today of 630,000 people.

   A. If this represents 17½% of the states population, how many people live in the state? Round all answers to the nearest whole person.

B. If the city's population today is 275% of what it was 10 years ago, how many people lived there 10 years ago?

C. Research indicates that in 5 years the population of the city will grow by 20.2%. Based on this prediction, how many people will be living there in 5 years?

33. At the end of the day, a fruit stand had total receipts of $1,249 in the cash register. If this included fruit sales and a 4% sales tax, how much of the receipts were from sales?

34. A manufacturing company has three departments—assembly, finishing, and packaging—with a total of 44,000 square feet. The assembly department has 15,400 square feet, the finishing department has 18,480 square feet, and the packaging department has the rest.
  A. What percent of the total square feet does each of the departments occupy?

  B. If the electricity bill for the plant amounted to $15,000 last month, what dollar amount of that bill should be allocated to each of the three departments, if the allocation is based on square footage?

35. An ice cream vendor pays $17.50 for a 5 gallon container of premium ice cream. From this quantity, he sells 80 scoops at $.90 per scoop. If he sold smaller scoops, he could sell 98 scoops from the same container; however, he could only charge $.80 per scoop. He has asked you, as his accountant, the following, "If I switch to the smaller scoops, will my profit per container go up or down, and by what percent?"

BUSINESS DECISION:
"Allocating Expenses at Fox's"

36. Daryl Fox owns three Burger King Restaurants with the following number of seats in each: airport, 340 seats; downtown, 218 seats; and suburban, 164 seats.

   A. If the liability insurance premium is $5,400 per year, how much of that premium should be allocated to each of the restaurants, based on percent of total seating capacity? (Round each percent to tenths.)

   B. If the restaurant chain opens a fourth location at the beach, with 150 seats, and the total insurance premium increases by 17%, what is the new allocation of insurance premiums among the four locations?

Course_____   Name _____
Term:_____   St #_____
Professor_____   Date:_____

A Little Math With Your Business
Assessment Test - Section II

Answer Sheet

1. _____	26. _____
2. _____	27. _____
3. _____	28. _____
4. _____	29A. _____
5. _____	29B. _____
6. _____	30. _____
7. _____	31A. _____
8. _____	31B. _____
9. _____	32A. _____
10. _____	32B. _____
11. _____	32C. _____
12. _____	33. _____
13. _____	34A. Assembly: _____
14. _____	Finishing: _____
15. _____	Packaging: _____
16. _____	34B. Assembly: _____
17. _____	Finishing: _____
18. _____	Packaging: _____
19. _____	35. _____
20. _____	36A. Airport: _____
21. _____	Downtown: _____
22. _____	Suburban: _____
23. _____	36B. Airport: _____
24. _____	Downtown: _____
25. Ethel: _____	Suburban: _____
Goldie: _____	Beach: _____

Section III

Business
Statistics
and
Data Presentation

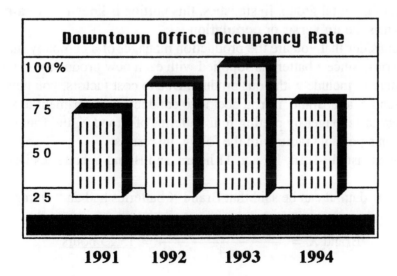

SECTION III

BUSINESS STATISTICS
AND
DATA PRESENTATION

INFORMATION, THE NAME OF THE GAME!

Statistical ideas and methods are found in almost every aspect of human activity, from the natural sciences to the social sciences. Statistics has special applications in such areas as medicine, psychology, education, engineering, and agriculture. In business today, statistical methods are applied extensively in production, marketing, finance, accounting, and many other areas involved in managerial decision making.

Understanding the meaning and implications of the numerical data generated by a company would be difficult without some knowledge of the subject of statistics. Numerical data form the raw material on which analyses, forecasts, and well-informed managerial plans and decisions are based. The major objective of statistics is to extract and present useful information from such data.

Business statistics is the systematic process of collecting, presenting, and interpreting numerical data about business situations. In business, statistics is organized into two categories, descriptive statistics and statistical inference. **Descriptive statistics** deals with the tabular or graphical "presentation" of data, while **statistical inference** is the process of arriving at conclusions, predictions, forecasts, or estimates about a total group under study, based on data obtained from only a portion of the total group. In statistics, this portion is known as a **sample,** and the total group is known as the **universe,** or **population.**

To illustrate, consider that you are the production manager of a company making products that use 9 volt batteries. Since a battery is supplied with each new product, you must determine which brand of battery to include with your product. Due to cost factors, you have narrowed the choice down to Brand X and Brand Y. You decide to conduct an experiment to see which of the two brands of battery lasts longer by putting four batteries of Brand X and four of Brand Y to a continuous use test in a portable radio with the following results:

Brand X batteries lasted 14, 16, 12, and 11 hours; and Brand Y batteries lasted 12, 13, 9, and 10 hours.

Based on this raw data, it can be said that Brand X batteries had an "average" duration of:

$$\text{Brand X} = \frac{14 + 16 + 12 + 11}{4} = \underline{13.25 \text{ hours}}$$

Brand Y batteries had an "average" duration of:

$$\text{Brand Y} = \frac{12 + 14 + 9 + 10}{4} = \underline{11.25 \text{ hours}}$$

The above experiment and calculations are a good example of descriptive statistics. Simple arithmetic was used to compute the two averages. These averages are "descriptive" of the two sets of data obtained from the test. To conclude from the experiment that "in general" Brand X batteries last longer than Brand Y puts the experiment into the realm of statistical inference. This supplement will be mainly concerned with descriptive statistics.

Statistics starts with the collection of raw data concerning a particular situation or question. For example, if management wanted the next annual report to present a comparison chart of company sales and profit figures with current industry standards, two types of information would be required. First, are the company records of sales and profits. This data would be readily available from **internal** company sources. Most large corporations today, using a vast array of computer systems, collect and store incredible amounts of information relating to all aspects of business activity. Management information systems then deliver this data, upon request, in an electronic moment.

Information gathered from sources outside the firm such as current industry statistics are known as **external** data, and are readily available from a variety of private, and government publications. The federal government is by far the largest researcher and publisher of business data. The Departments of Commerce and Labor periodically publish information relating to all aspects of the economy and the country. Some of these publications are the *Statistical Abstract of the United States, Survey of Current Business, Monthly Labor Review, Federal Reserve Bulletin, Census of the United States,* and the *Census of Business.*

Private statistical services such as Moody's Investors Service and Standard and Poor's offer a wealth of information for business decision making. Other private sources are periodicals such as *The Wall Street Journal, Fortune, Business Week, Forbes,* and *Money,* as well as hundreds of industry and trade publications.

MEASURES OF CENTRAL TENDENCY

A numerical **average** is a value that typifies, or is representative of, a whole range of values. Since an average is numerically located within the range of values that it represents, the various types of averages are often referred to as measures of central tendency. In this section we shall consider the three most commonly used averages in business statistics: the arithmetic mean, the median, and the mode.

Arithmetic Mean

The arithmetic mean corresponds to the generally accepted meaning of the word "average." It is customary to abbreviate the term arithmetic mean and refer to this average simply as the **mean.** The mean is found by taking the sum of a set of values and dividing this sum by the number of values.

$$\text{arithmetic mean} = \frac{\text{Sum of values}}{\text{Number of values}}$$

EXAMPLE 1

If a hardware store had daily sales of $4,635 on Monday, $3,655 on Tuesday, $3,506 on Wednesday, $2,870 on Thursday, $4,309 on Friday, and $5,475 on Saturday, what is the average sales per day?

SOLUTION STRATEGY _____

To calculate the mean (average sales per day), we find the sum of the values (sales per day), and divide this sum by the number of values (6 days).

$$\text{average sales per day} = \frac{4{,}635 + 3{,}655 + 3{,}506 + 2{,}870 + 4{,}309 + 5{,}475}{6} = \frac{24{,}450}{6} = \$4{,}075 \text{ per day}$$

TRY-IT EXERCISE

1. The attendance figures for a series of management seminars are as follows: 433, 247, 661, 418, and 512. What was the average number of people attending per seminar?

Check your answer with the correct answers and worked-out solutions in the appendix.

Median

The **median** of a set of numbers is the "midpoint" value when the numbers are ranked in assending or descending order. When there are an odd number of values in the set, the middle value is the median. For example, in a set of seven ranked values, the fourth value is the midpoint; three values above, and three values below the median.

When there are an even number of values in the set, the median is the midpoint between the two middle values. For example, in a set with 10 values, the median would be the midpoint between the fifth and the sixth value.

EXAMPLE 2

Find the median for the following set of values:

2   8   5   13   11   6   9   15   4

SOLUTION STRATEGY _____

First, rank the data as follows: 2 4 5 6 8 9 11 13 15. Since the number of values in the set is nine, there will be four values below and four values above the median. This makes the median the fifth value, in this case <u>8</u>.

EXAMPLE 3

Find the median for the following set of values:

56   34   87   12   45   49

SOLUTION STRATEGY_____

Once again, we rank the data, 12   34   45   49   56   87. Since the number of values in this set is six, the median is the midpoint between the third and the fourth values, 45 and 49.

$$\text{median} = \frac{45 + 49}{2} = \frac{94}{2} = \underline{47}$$

The median is a more useful measure of central tendency than the mean when one or more of the values of the set is significantly higher or lower than the rest of the set. For example, if five people were ages 22, 26, 27, 31, and 69, we see that the mean of this set is 35, whereas the median is 27, a number "more descriptive" of the set.

Range

The **range,** another useful measure in statistics, is the difference between the lowest and the highest values in a set. In the set of ages, above, the range would be $69 - 22 = \underline{47}$.

TRY-IT EXERCISES

2. Calculate the median and the range for the following sets of data:
   A. 12   33   42   13   79   29   101   54   76   81

   B. 4,589   6,558   4,237   2,430   3,619   5,840   1,220

Check your answers with the correct answers and worked-out solutions in the appendix.

Mode

The **mode** is the third measure of central tendency we shall consider. It is the value or values in a set that occur most often. If all values appear only once, there is no mode. When more than one value occurs the same number of times then there are more than one mode. The mode is useful in merchandising to keep track of the most frequently purchased goods.

EXAMPLE 4

What is the mode of the following set of values representing wattage of lightbulb sales in a hardware store:

25 25 60 60 60 75 75 75 75 100 100 150

SOLUTION STRATEGY_____

From this data we see that the mode is 75 watt bulbs. This would indicate to the retailer that this was the most frequently purchased lightbulb. Calculating the mean and median of this set of data would provide little useful information.

TRY-IT EXERCISE

3. Calculate the mode of the following set of values representing the size, in gallons, of fish tanks sold in a pet shop:

10 10 20 10 55 20 10 65 85 20 10 20 55 10 125 55 10 20

Check your answer with the correct answers and worked-out solutions in the appendix.

FREQUENCY DISTRIBUTIONS

In the previous examples, the values in the sets were listed individually and are known as **ungrouped data.** Frequently, business statistics deals with hundreds or even thousands of values in a set. In dealing with such a large amount of values it is often easier to "represent" the data by dividing the values into equal size groups known as classes, thus the term **grouped data.** The number of values in each class is called the **frequency,** with the resulting chart called a **frequency table.** To construct a frequency table, divide the data into equal size classes and use tally marks to record the frequency of values within each class.

After the data has been grouped, multiply the frequency for each class by the midpoint of that class. The **mean of grouped data** is found by the formula:

$$\text{Mean of grouped data} = \frac{\text{sum of (frequency} \times \text{midpoint)}}{\text{sum of frequency}}$$

EXAMPLE 5

From the following ungrouped data, representing the weight of packages shipped by your company this month, construct a frequency table using classes with an interval of 10 pounds each and calcuate the mean of the grouped data rounded to the nearest tenth of a pound.

13 16 65 45 44 35 22 46 36 49 56 26
68 27 35 15 43 62 32 57 48 23 43 44

SOLUTION STRATEGY_____

First we find the **range** of the data by subtracting the lowest value, 13, from the highest value, 68. This gives a range of 55 pounds. By using 60 pounds as the range for our frequency table we are sure to include all values in the set. Class intervals of 10 pounds each allows for 6 equal classes:

CLASS (lbs)	TALLY	FREQUENCY (f)	MIDPOINT (m)	f × m
10 to 20	111	3	15	45
20 to 30	1111	4	25	100
30 to 40	1111	4	35	140
40 to 50	⌊⌊⌊⌊ 111	8	45	360
50 to 60	11	2	55	110
60 to 70	111	3	65	195
		24		950

From this frequency table, we can now calculate the mean of the grouped data:

$$\text{Mean of grouped data} = \frac{\text{sum of (frequency} \times \text{midpoint)}}{\text{sum of frequency}} = \frac{950}{24} = \underline{39.6 \text{ lbs.}}$$

TRY-IT EXERCISE

4. From the following ungrouped data, representing the dollar sales of each transaction in a clothing boutique, construct a frequency table using classes with an interval of 10 dollars each and calculate the mean of the grouped data.

   14 19 55 47 44 39 22 71 35 49 64 22 88 78 16
   88 37 29 71 74 62 54 59 18 93 49 74 26 66 75

Check your answer with the correct answers and worked-out solutions in the appendix.

DATA PRESENTATION

In business statistics, tables and graphs are used extensively to summarize and display data in a clear and concise manner, as well as to help interpret and communicate numerical facts. The three found most commonly in business are the line graph, the bar graph, and the circle graph.

Line Graph

The **line graph** shows data changing over a period of time. The horizontal or x-axis is usually used to measure units of time, such as weeks, months, or years, while the vertical or y-axis depicts measurements such as sales dollars or production units. Frequently the y-axis is used to measure the percentage of something.

Line graphs are actually a series of "data points" on a grid, continuously connected by straight lines. They may contain a single line, representing the "change" of one variable, such as interest rates; or they may contain multiple lines representing the change of interrelated variables such as interest rates and stock prices, or sales and profits. Below are examples of two line graphs from the textbook.

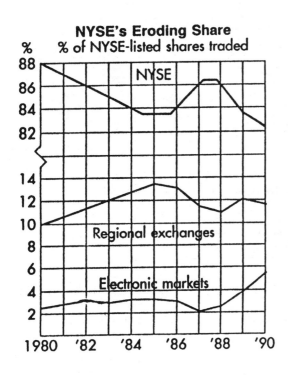

Figure 21.8
Reported Share Volume for NYSE

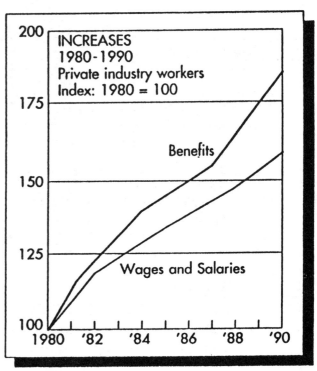

Figure 11.7
Increasing Costs of Employee Benefits

Bar Graphs

The **bar graph** represents data by the length of horizontal bars or vertical columns. As with line graphs, bar graphs often illustrate increases or decreases in magnitude of a certain variable. Bar graphs may or may not be based on the movement of time. Below is an example of a standard bar graph from the textbook.

Figure 6.2   Greatest Financial Obstacles of Small Businesses

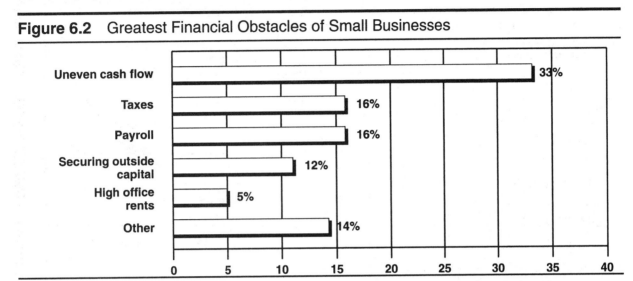

A **component bar graph** is used to illustrate parts of something, which add to a total. Each bar is divided into the components, "stacked" on top of each other, and shaded or colored differently. For example, if a company sells three different models of a certain product, the component bar graph could be used to show the monthly total sales of that product, with the bar divided into segments representing each model. Below is an example of a component bar graph from the textbook.

Figure 7.1   Types of Skills Needed at Each Level of Management

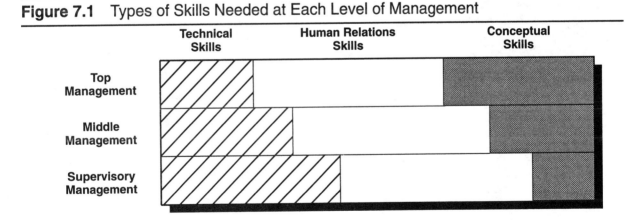

A **comparative bar graph** is used to illustrate two or more related variables. In this graph, the bars of the related variables are drawn next to each other. As with the single bar graph, the x-axis may or may not depict time. The bars representing each variable should be shaded or colored differently to make the graph easy to read and interpret. Below is an example of a comparative bar graph from the textbook.

Figure 11.8 Comparison of Fixed and Flexible Employee Benefit Plans

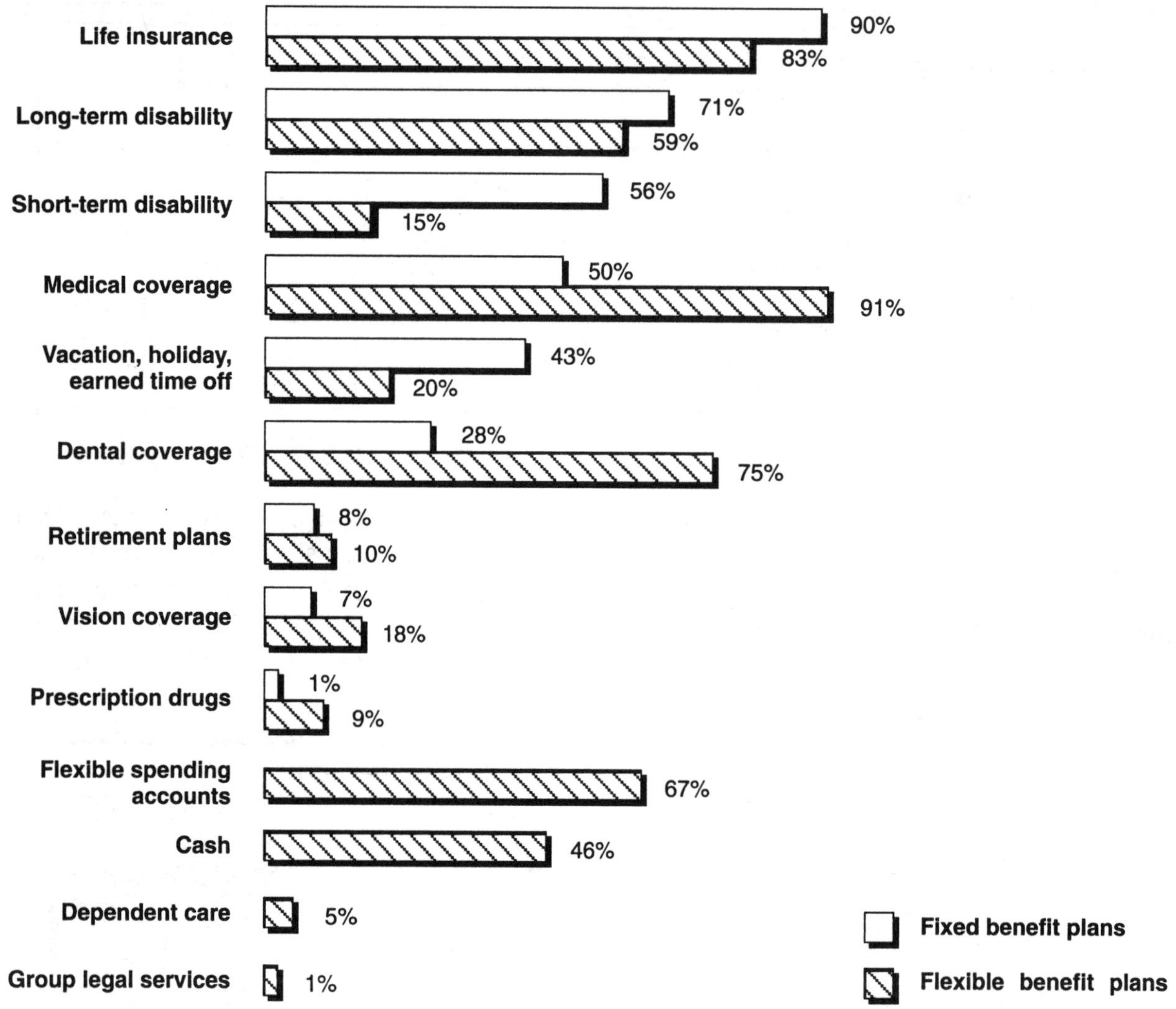

Life insurance — 90% / 83%
Long-term disability — 71% / 59%
Short-term disability — 56% / 15%
Medical coverage — 50% / 91%
Vacation, holiday, earned time off — 43% / 20%
Dental coverage — 28% / 75%
Retirement plans — 8% / 10%
Vision coverage — 7% / 18%
Prescription drugs — 1% / 9%
Flexible spending accounts — 67%
Cash — 46%
Dependent care — 5%
Group legal services — 1%

Fixed benefit plans
Flexible benefit plans

Circle Graph

The **circle graph,** or **pie chart,** is one or more circles divided into sections representing the component parts of a whole in percentage terms. The whole, 100%, is the circle; the parts are the wedge-shaped sections of the circle. When this type of graph is used, the data are converted to percentages. The size of each section of the circle is determined by the fractional equivalent of the percent, such as 25% = ¼ of the circle, or 50% = ½ of the circle. Below are two examples of circle graphs from the textbook.

Figure 10.8   The Changing U.S. Population: 1991–2021

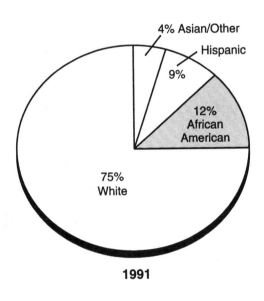

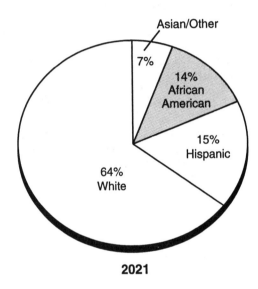

Student Notes

Section III
Assessment Test
(Use the Answer Sheet provided at the end of this test.)

1. You have just been hired as the quality control manager for Bayside Manufacturing, a company producing electronic components for computer systems. Top management has requested a status report on the number of "defective" units produced each day. You decide to keep track of the number of defects each day for a month, 30 days. The following are the results of your survey:
    Bayside Manufacturing – Defects per day – Survey 1

    11, 13, 17, 13, 15, 9, 14, 11, 13, 15, 11, 10, 13, 11, 15,
    19, 15, 13, 15, 9, 11, 19, 20, 13, 15, 18, 12, 11, 14, 16

    A. Find the mean, the median, and the mode of this data for your report to top management.

    After implementing your suggestions for improved quality on the production line, you decide to survey the defects for another 30 days, with the following results:
    Bayside Manufacturing – Defects per day – Survey 2

    11, 9, 12, 7, 8, 11, 10, 13, 9, 9, 11, 12, 8, 10, 11,
    7, 9, 11, 9, 6, 12, 10, 9, 8, 12, 10, 11, 9, 7, 10

    B. Find the mean, the median, and the mode of the new data.

    C. If defective units cost the company $42.50 each to fix, use the "means" to find the average cost per day for defects, before and after your improvements?

D. Theoretically, how much will your improvements save the company in a 250-day production year?

E. Congratulations! The company has awarded you a bonus amounting to 15% of the first year savings. How much is your bonus check?

2.   You are the general manager of a chain of four clothing boutique shops located in large shopping malls in your city. The following chart shows the quarterly (13 week) sales in thousands of dollars for each of the stores last year:

	1st Quarter	2nd Quarter	3rd Quarter	4th Quarter
Adventure Mall	225	214	194	237
Lakeside Mall	154	139	132	166
Sunshine Mall	268	254	259	311
Hawaiian Mall	127	121	119	144

A. What is the mean quarterly sales for each of the stores?

B. What is the mean sales for each of the four quarters?

3.   You are the personnel director for the Lambert Corporation. Forty applicants for employment were given an assessment test in math and English with the following results:

```
87  76  81  93  55  49  72  84  68  33
57  79  83  94  46  93  84  82  75  27
69  57  66  81  87  12  76  54  78  98
68  56  73  79  74  92  53  85  82  75
```

A. Calculate the mean of the ungrouped data.

B. Group the data into 10 classes of equal size (1–10, 11–20, 21–30, 31–40, etc.), and construct a frequency distribution showing all tally marks.

C. Calculate the mean of the grouped data, using 5, 15, 25, 35, 45, etc., as the midpoints.

D. If company policy is to consider only those who score 10 points higher than the mean of the grouped data or better, how many from this group are still being considered for the job?

4.   The following data represent the ages of the employees in your company.

```
23  43  24  65  45  33  53  51  42  22  39  55
36  49  28  63  46  30  46  37  31  48  36  22
41  59  60  45  41  24  33  53  29  26  62  50
```

A. What is the mean of the ungrouped data?

B. Create a frequency distribution with tally marks of the ages using the classes: 21–30, 31–40, etc.

C. Construct a bar graph of the data. Use the horizontal or x-axis for the age classes, and the vertical or y-axis for the frequency of each class.

5.   The following data represents the monthly sales figures for the New York and California branches of the Rand Corporation.

	January	February	March	April	May	June
New York:	$121,000	$254,000	$218,000	$176,000	$155,000	$210,000
California:	$ 98,000	$125,000	$211,000	$225,000	$240,000	$250,000

A. Construct a line graph depicting the monthly sales for the two branches. Show the New York branch as a solid line and the California branch as a dotted line.

B. Construct a comparative bar graph for the same data. Highlight the bars differently for each branch.

6.   Last month Computers USA sold $150,000 in standard computers, $75,000 in portable computers, $30,000 in software, $37,500 in printers, and $7,500 in other accessories.
A. What percent of the total sales does each category of merchandise represent?

B. Construct a circle graph depicting the percentage breakdown of sales for Computers USA.

BUSINESS DECISION:
'Beat the Mean' Bonus

7. You are the owner of Supreme Imports, Inc., a used car dealership specializing in expensive pre-owned automobiles, such as Mercedes Benz, BMW, Lexus, and the like. You have a unique and quite motivating bonus plan that has worked very well over the years.

Each quarter the mean number of cars sold is calculated. The first time a salesperson sells more cars than the mean, they earn a $100 bonus for each car *over the mean* in that quarter. If a salesperson beats the mean a second time in a year, the bonus increases to $150 per car for that quarter. Three times over the mean in one year and the bonus is $200 per car for that quarter. If anyone beats the mean all four quarters, the fourth quarter bonus is $300 per car. Remember, the bonus is paid only for the number of cars *over* the mean.

Each year the program starts all over again. All bonuses are paid once per year, in January, for the previous year. The following table represents the number of cars sold by your five salespeople, each quarter last year.

	First Quarter	Second Quarter	Third Quarter	Fourth Quarter
Evans:	16	23	14	23
Chen:	12	20	16	25
Walker:	15	13	26	19
Black:	22	20	27	19
Sanchez:	25	19	32	24

Calculate how much bonus each person should receive for last year.

Evans:

Chen:

Walker:

Black:

Sanchez:

Course_____   Name_____
Term:_____   St #_____
Professor_____   Date:_____

A Little Math With Your Business
Assessment Test - Section III
Answer Sheet

1A.   Survey 1:
         Mean _____
         Median _____
         Mode _____

1B.   Survey 2:
         Mean _____
         Median _____
         Mode _____

1C.   Cost per day:
         Before _____
         After _____

1D.   _____

1E.   _____

2A.   Mean quarterly sales: (000)
         Adventure _____
         Lakeside _____
         Sunshine _____
         Hawaiian _____

2B.   Mean quarterly sales: (000)
         1st qtr _____
         2nd qtr _____
         3rd qtr _____
         4th qtr _____

3A.   _____
3B.   Use separate sheet
3C.   _____
3D.   _____
4A.   _____
4B.   Use separate sheet
4C.   Use separate sheet
5A.   Use separate sheet

5B.   Use separate sheet
6A.   Percent of sales:
         Standard _____
         Portable _____
         Software _____
         Printers _____
         Accessories _____

6B.   Use separate sheet

7.   Evans: _____
         Chen: _____
         Walker: _____
         Black: _____
         Sanchez: _____

Section IV

Business
Measurements,
Currency Conversion,
and the
Metric System

SECTION IV

BUSINESS MEASUREMENTS, CURRENCY CONVERSION, AND THE METRIC SYSTEM

Measuring is the act of assigning a number to a quantity of "something" in order to represent its magnitude. It is one of the connecting links between mathematics and the physical world. Historically, units of measurement were related to various parts of the human body. The **cubit** was the length of the forearm from the elbow to the end of the middle finger, about 18 inches. The **foot** was said to be the length of a king's foot, varying over the years from 9 to 18 inches. Two steps of a soldier was a **pace,** and 1,000 paces was a mile. The weight of a pint of ale was called a **pound,** and thus the old saying, "A pint is a pound, the world around." As technology and trade progressed over time, more accurate and permanent **standard units** were established for weights and measures.

Measurements are used in all aspects of business activity on a daily basis. Builders, architects, designers, and decorators are involved with measures of length and area. Warehouse managers and those involved in shipping and handling of goods use weight and capacity calculations constantly. Managers of wholesale and retail businesses use surface measures such as floor space and shelf space allocations. In business, these calculations are often combined with dollar amounts to arrive at price per unit of measure, such as cost per square foot. Production lines use measurements of all kinds to manufacture an endless variety of products.

Until recently, the United States primarily recognized a cumbersome system of weights and measures known as the **U. S. customary** or **English system.** This system, brought to America by the colonists, uses the now familiar units of yards, feet, and inches for length; ounces, pounds, and tons for dry weight; and ounces, pints, quarts, and gallons for liquid measure. In 1971, the U. S. began a gradual transition to a system used by most of the civilized world known as the **metric system.** Although it was legalized for commerce and trade in 1866, the metric system has not been widely accepted in this country.

From Chapter 3 in your textbook, The Global Dimensions of Business, we find that more and more American companies are doing business overseas, and more and more foreign companies are doing business in the U. S. It is understandable, therefore, that all the countries of the world economic community recognize and use the same system of measurements.

Aimed at helping U. S. industries stay competitive, the latest official action regarding metrics is a little-noticed provision within the American Technology Pre-eminence Act, signed into law on February 14, 1992. The legislation includes amendments to the Fair Packaging & Labeling Act, requiring all packaging and labeling to use metric measurements for net quantities "as the primary system for measuring quantity" by February 1994. The use of ounces and pounds, now commonly used as measurements, will become optional.

Part I of this section deals with the U. S. customary, or English system. It will be many years before these measurements are no longer used in this country. Today's business person should still have a working knowledge of this system.

Part II, Going International, deals with the conversion between four important currencies of the world: the United States Dollar, the Japanese Yen, the British Pound, and the German Deutsche Mark.

Part III covers the metric system of measurement and the conversions between the U. S. and the metric systems. It is important for you to be able to use the tables in this section to solve measurement problems, and readily convert from one system to the other. Don't memorize the conversions—just remember where you put the tables!

PART I   U. S. CUSTOMARY SYSTEM

The following measurement and conversion tables are for the U. S. customary system. They are separated into the categories of linear or straight measure; surface or square measure; volume, liquid, and dry measure; weight measure; and time measure.

The measurement tables are a complete listing for each category, while the conversion tables are for the most commonly used units. After looking them over, you will probably find that many of them are already familiar to you. Use the tables to solve the Try-It Exercises at the end of each category. Your answers should be rounded to the nearest tenths.

MEASUREMENT TABLES

Linear or Straight Measure

U. S. Customary Unit	U. S. Equivalents
inch (in.)	.083 foot
foot (ft.)	⅓ yard, 12 inches
yard (yd.)	3 feet, 36 inches
rod (rd.)	5½ yards, 16½ feet
furlong (fur.)	⅛ mile, 220 yards
mile (mi.) statute, land	1,760 yards, 5,280 feet
mile (nm.) nautical, sea	1.151 statute miles

Conversion Factors - LENGTH

To convert from	To	Multiply
Feet	inches	number of feet by 12
Yards	inches	number of yards by 36
Yards	feet	number of yards by 3
Miles	feet	number of miles by 5280

To convert from	To	Divide
Inches	feet	number of inches by 12
Inches	yards	number of inches by 36
Feet	yards	number of feet by 3
Feet	miles	number of feet by 5280

TRY-IT EXERCISES - Length

Convert each of the following measurements, as indicated:

1. 105 ft. = _____ yd.

2. 156 in. = _____ ft.

3. 2.4 mi. = _____ ft.

4. 8½ ft. = _____ in.

5. 432 in. = _____ yd.

6. 11 yd. = _____ ft.

7. 23,760 ft. = _____ mi.

8. 3¼ yd. = _____ in.

9. On a flight from Dallas to San Francisco, the pilot announces that the plane will be flying at 35,000 ft. How many miles high is the plane? (Round to the nearest tenth of a mile.)

10. If a runner has a pace of 4 ft. 3 in., how many paces will be required to run a 3 mile race?

Check your answers with the correct answers and worked-out solutions in the appendix.

Surface or Square Measure

U. S. Customary Unit	U. S. Equivalents
square inch (sq. in.)	0.007 square feet
square foot (sq. ft.)	144 square inches
square yard (sq. yd.)	1,296 square inches 9 square feet
acre (a.)	43,560 square feet 4.840 square yards
square mile (sq. mi.)	640 acres

Conversion Factors - SURFACE

To convert from	To	Multiply
Square feet	square inches	number of sq. ft. by 144
Square yards	square feet	number of sq. yd. by 9
Acres	square yards	number of acres by 4,840
Square miles	acres	number of sq. mi. by 640

To convert from	To	Divide
Square inches	square feet	number of sq. inches by 144
Square feet	square yards	number of sq. feet by 9
Square yards	acres	number of sq. yards by 4,840
Acres	square miles	number of acres by 640

TRY-IT EXERCISES - Surface Area

Convert each of the following measurements, as indicated:

11. 540 sq. in. = _____ sq. ft.

12. 51 acres = _____ sq. yd.

13. 980 sq. yd. = _____ sq. ft.

14. 81,280 acres = _____ sq. mi.

15. 10,648 sq. yd. = _____ acres

16. 240 sq. ft. = _____ sq. in.

17. 2½ sq. mi. = _____ acres

18. 774 sq. ft. = _____ sq. yd.

19. How many square miles is a ranch containing 5,696 acres of land?

20. A room measures 15 feet in length and 18 feet in width. Using the formula area = length × width, (A = LW)
   A. How many square feet are in the room?

   B. How many square yards of carpeting will be required to cover the floor?

   C. If the carpeting chosen costs $18.55 per square yard, the padding $.75 per square foot, and the labor $200, what is the total cost to carpet the room?

Check your answers with the correct answers and worked-out solutions in the appendix.

Volume or Capacity
Measure

U. S. Customary Unit	U. S. Equivalents
cubic inch (cu. in.)	0.00058 cubic foot
cubic foot (cu. ft.)	1,728 cubic inches
cubic yard (cu. yd.)	27 cubic feet

Liquid Measure

U. S. Customary	U. S. Equivalents
fluid ounce (fl. oz.)	8 fluid drams
pint (pt.)	6 fluid ounces
quart (qt.)	2 pints
gallon (gal.)	4 quarts
barrel (bbl.)	varies from 31 to 42 gallons

Dry Measure

U. S. Customary	U. S. Equivalents
pint (pt.)	½ quart
quart (qt.)	2 pints
peck (pk.)	8 quarts
bushel (bu.)	4 pecks

Conversion Factors - Volume, Liquid & Dry Measure

	To convert from		To	Multiply
Volume		Cubic feet	cubic inches	number of cu. ft. by 1,728
		Cubic yards	cubic feet	number of cu. yd. by 27
Liquid		Pints	fluid ounces	number of pints by 16
		Quarts	pints	number of quarts by 2
		Gallons	quarts	number of gallons by 4
Dry		Quarts	pints	number of quarts by 2
		Pecks	quarts	number of pecks by 8
		Bushels	pecks	number of bushels by 4
	To convert from		To	Divide
Volume		Cubic inches	cubic feet	number of cu. in. by 1,728
		Cubic feet	cubic yards	number of cu. ft. by 27
Liquid		Fluid ounces	pints	number of fl. oz. by 16
		Pints	quarts	number of pints by 2
		Quarts	gallons	number of quarts by 4
Dry		Pints	quarts	number of pints by 2
		Quarts	pecks	number of quarts by 8
		pecks	bushels	number of pecks by 4

TRY-IT EXERCISES - Volume, Liquid & Dry Measure

Convert each of the following measurements, as indicated:

21. 80 fl. oz. = _____ pints

22. 12 pecks = _____ qts.

23. 7 cu. yd. = _____cu. ft.

24. 12,960 cu. in. = _____ cu. ft.

25. 51 qts. = _____ pecks

26. 19.6 gal. = _____ qts.

27. 33½ pts. = _____ qts.

28. 41 bushels = _____ pecks

29. A small motor assembly line uses 2.6 pints of oil per motor. If the plant produces 35 motors per shift, and runs 2 shifts per day, 5 days per week,
   A. How many gallons of oil are used in a 7-week production run?

   B. If oil costs the company $.77 per quart, what is the total cost of the oil?

30. A large grocery store purchases a bushel of strawberries for $45. If the store sells them for $1.19 per pint, how much gross profit do they make per bushel?

Check your answers with the correct answers and worked-out solutions in the appendix.

Avoirdupois Weight

U. S. Customary Unit	U. S. Equivalents
grain (gr.)	0.036 dram
dram (dr.)	27.344 grains
ounce (oz.)	16 drams
pound (lb.)	16 ounces 7,000 grains
hundredweight (cwt.)	100 pounds
ton, short (t.)	2,000 pounds
ton, long	1.12 short tons 2,240 pounds

Conversion Factors - WEIGHT

To convert from	To	Multiply
Pounds	ounces	number of lbs. by 16
Tons (short)	pounds	number of tons by 2,000
Tons (long)	pounds	number of tons by 2,240

To convert from	To	Divide
Ounces	pounds	number of oz. by 16
Pounds	tons (short)	number of lbs. by 2,000
Pounds	tons (long)	number of lbs. by 2,240

TRY-IT EXERCISES - Weight

Convert each of the following measurements, as indicated:

31. 36 oz. = _____ lb.

32. 14 lb. = _____ oz.

33. 4.2 t. (short) = _____lb.

34. 49,280 lb. = _____ t. (long)

35. 656 oz. = _____ lb.

36. 127½ lb. = _____ oz.

37. 3,400 lb. = _____ t. (short)

38. .75 lb. = _____oz.

39. If John weighed 173 lb. 12 oz., and Sam weighed 88 oz. less, how much does Sam weigh?

40. A truck weighs 4,550 lb. empty, and carries a load of gravel weighing 10,300 lb. If a road sign before a bridge reads, "Trucks, 8½ Ton Limit,"
A. Is it safe for the truck to cross the bridge?

B. By how many pounds was it safe, or not?

Check your answers with the correct answers and worked-out solutions in the appendix.

Time

Standard Units	Equivalents
minute (min.)	60 seconds
hour (hr.)	60 minutes
day (da.)	24 hours
week (wk.)	7 days
month (mo.)	4⅓ weeks
quarter (qtr.)	13 weeks
year (yr.)	4 quarters 12 months 52 weeks 365 days, 366 leap year
decade	10 years
century	10 decades 100 years

Conversion Factors - TIME

To convert from	To	Multiply
Minutes	seconds	number of minutes by 60
Hours	minutes	number of hours by 60
Days	hours	number of days by 24
Weeks	days	number of weeks by 7

To convert from	To	Divide
Seconds	minutes	number of seconds by 60
Minutes	hours	number of minutes by 60
Hours	days	number of hours by 24
Days	weeks	number of days by 7

TRY-IT EXERCISES - **Time**

Convert each of the following measurements, as indicated:

41. 36 hrs. = _____ da.

42. 2.5 min. = _____ sec.

43. 63 da. = _____wk.

44. 1¼ hr. = _____ min.

45. 150 min. = _____ hr.

46. 210 sec. = _____ min.

47. 12 wk. = _____ da.

48. 33 mo. = _____ yr.

49. You have just received a loan from the Benevolent Bank for 66 months.
   A. For how many years is this loan?

   B. If your first monthly payment starts on April 1 of the current year, what is the date of your final payment?

50. You are a pilot in training. Yesterday you spent from 2:45 PM until 4:18 PM in a flight simulator practicing for your final flight check. If the simulator cost $1.70 per minute to rent, how much did the practice session cost?

Check your answers with the correct answers and worked-out solutions in the appendix.

PART II CURRENCY CONVERSION—GOING INTERNATIONAL!

With more and more American companies, both large and small, doing business in other countries, understanding how currency is converted has become an increasingly important business math skill. United States dollars are legal currency only in the U. S. To travel abroad, or to buy goods from other countries, dollars must be exchanged for foreign currency.

Until recently, exchange rates between important currencies were **fixed,** with sudden, large changes forced only by the pressures of world events. Eventually these pressures became too great and too persistent, so rates now **vary** on a daily basis among major currencies. The system is known as **floating exchange rates.**

Although there are over 50 currencies being used in international trade today, our discussion will focus on 4 major ones:

COUNTRY	CURRENCY	SYMBOL
United States	Dollar	$
United Kingdom	Pound	£
Japan	Yen	¥
Germany	Deutsche Mark	DM

Once you have gained an understanding of how these currencies are converted, the technique can be applied to any currencies in the world.

Below is a **"Currency Cross Rate"** chart showing the current exchange rates between important currencies. These exchange rates are really "Multiplier" factors used to convert one currency to another. These charts can be found daily in most major newspapers' financial sections.

Currency Cross Rates

For Each

	U. S. $	U. K. £	Japanese ¥	German DM
YOU GET				
German DM	1.5385 DM	2.9243 DM	.01285 DM	
Japanese ¥	¥123.87	¥227.57		¥77.821
U. K. £	£.64550		£.00439	£.34196
U. S. $		$1.5605	$.00812	$.65120

The four columns: U. S. $, U. K. £, Japanese ¥, and German DM, represent the currency you have now. As you look down the column you will see the equivalent amount of the other currency (multiplier), which you will receive for 1 unit of your currency.

As you look down the U. S. dollar column, column 1 of the chart, you see that one U. S. dollar converts to 1.5385 DM, ¥123.87, and £.64550. These exchange rates are then multiplied times the number of U. S. dollars to be converted.

EXAMPLE

You are a sales representative of a company that sells motor parts in many countries. You are going on a selling trip to Japan next week. The company has allotted $2,550 for expenses during your stay in Japan. You decide to convert the money to Japanese yen. Based on the "Currency Cross Rates" chart:

A. How many yen will you have for the trip?

B. Upon returning to the U. S. you still have ¥56,700. Convert those yen back to dollars.

SOLUTION STRATEGY _____

A. Since you are holding U. S. dollars, look down column 1 of the chart to Japanese ¥. Note that the exchange rate is ¥123.87 for every dollar.

Next, multiply the number of dollars times the exchange rate:

$$2,550 \times ¥123.87 = \underline{¥315,868.5}$$

B. Since you are now holding Japanese yen and want to convert them to U. S. dollars, look down column 3 of the chart to U. S. $. Note that the exchange rate is $.00812 for every yen.

Next, multiply the number of yen times the exchange rate:

$$56,700 \times \$.00812 = \underline{\$460.40}$$

TRY-IT EXERCISES - **Currency Conversion**

Convert each of the following as indicated:

51. $360 to pounds. _____

52. ¥18,400 to Deutsche marks. _____

53. £4,500 to yen. _____

54. 300 DM to dollars. _____

55. Your company is sending you on a business trip to England. Your expense account will be $1,500.

A. How many pounds will that convert to?

B. Upon your return, you have £133 left over. How many dollars will this convert to?

Check your answers with the correct answers and worked-out solutions in the appendix.

PART III   THE METRIC SYSTEM

The standard international metric system of measurement, known as SI, is a decimal system, based on the number 10, and is one of the easiest and most useful measuring systems ever established. The metric system was developed by a group of scientists after the French Revolution in 1789. Although it was slow to be accepted for many years, by 1875 it was adopted as the international standard of weights and measures.

The metric system is divided into three basic units, the meter, the liter, and the gram. The **meter (m)** is the basic unit of length, and is slightly longer than a yard. The **liter (l)** is the basic unit of volume and is slightly larger than a quart. The **gram (g)** is the basic unit of weight and is about $\frac{1}{28}$ of an ounce. A penny weighs about 2½ grams.

The metric system uses a series of prefixes to designate quantities larger or smaller than the basic units. Each quantity is a factor of 10 of the preceding prefix.

For numbers **larger** than the basic unit we use the prefixes:

deca- (dk)	10 times the basic unit	Example: 1 decameter (dkm) = 10 meters
hecto- (h)	100 times the basic unit	Example: 1 hectoliter (hl) = 100 liters
kilo- (k)	1000 times the basic unit	Example: 1 kilogram (kg) = 1000 grams

For numbers **smaller** than the basic unit we use the prefixes:

deci- (d)	1/10 of the basic unit	Example: 1 deciliter (dl) = .01 of a liter
centi- (c)	1/100 of the basic unit	Example: 1 centimeter (cm) = .001 of a meter
milli- (m)	1/1000 of the basic unit	Example: 1 milligram (mg) = .0001 of a gram

Since the metric system is based on decimals, we can convert to larger and smaller units by moving the decimal point to the right and to the left. Each "place" the decimal moves to the right is the same as multiplying by 10. Each "place" the decimal moves to the left is the same as dividing by 10.

By using the chart below and the following steps, we can easily convert between metric measurements:

Steps for converting metrics to metrics:

1. Count the "places" between the two prefixes being converted.
2. Move the decimal point that number of "places" to the left or right.

kilo-	**hecto-**	**deca-**	**Basic Unit**	**deci-**	**centi-**	**milli-**
			(meter, liter, gram)			

EXAMPLE

Convert 3.57 kilometers to meters.

SOLUTION STRATEGY _____

From the chart we see that a conversion from kilometers to the basic unit meters is a move of three places to the right:

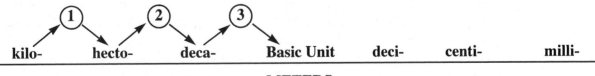

METERS

Therefore, to convert a distance of 3.57 kilometers to meters, we move the decimal point three places to the right,

3.57 km = 3,570 m

EXAMPLE

Convert 550,300 milligrams to kilograms.

SOLUTION STRATEGY_____

From the chart, we see that a conversion from milligrams to kilograms is a move of six places to the left:

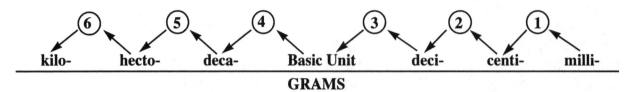

Therefore, to convert a weight of 550,300 mg to kilograms, we move the decimal point six places to the left,

$$550,300 \text{ mg} = \underline{0.5503 \text{ kg}}$$

TRY-IT EXERCISES - **Metric to Metric Conversions**

Length - Volume - Weight

Convert each of the following, as indicated:

56. 32 cm = _____ m   **57.** 57 mm = _____ cm   **58.** 38 km = _____ m

59. 507 m = _____ cm   **60.** 12.5 kg = _____ g   **61.** 9 g = _____ mg

62. 24 hg = _____ dg   **63.** 6.7 l = _____ ml   **64.** 569 cl = _____ l

65. 383 ml = _____ l   **66.** 1,800 g = _____ kg   **67.** 148 cm = _____ m

Check your answers with the correct answers and worked-out solutions in the appendix.

OTHER METRIC CONVERSIONS

Surface Area

In the metric system, the basic unit for surface measure is the square meter. Remember, when measuring surface area, we use the formula area = length × width. 100 square meters equal an **are (a).** An are is a surface measure of 10 meters by 10 meters. A unit known as a **hectare (ha),** is equal to 10,000 square meters, or a surface area of 100 meters by 100 meters. A hectare is approximately 2.5 acres.

Conversion Factors		
To convert from	**To**	**Multiply**
Ares	square meters	number of ares by 100
Hectares	ares	number of hectares by 100
Hectares	square meters	number of hectares by 10,000
To convert from	**To**	**Divide**
Square meters	ares	number of square meters by 100
Square meters	hectares	number of square meters by 10,000
Ares	hectares	number of ares by 10

Temperature

The U. S. customary system measures temperature in degrees **Fahrenheit (F),** while the metric system uses degrees **Centigrade,** or **Celsius (C).** Notice that the word centigrade has the prefix "centi-" meaning 100. The Celsius temperature scale is based on 100 degrees from freezing to boiling of water, although the word centigrade is no longer used as a metric measurement.

To convert from Fahrenheit to Celsius, use the formula:

$$C = \tfrac{5}{9} (F - 32)$$

To convert from Celsius to Fahrenheit, use the formula:

$$F = 1.8C + 32$$

| TRY-IT EXERCISES | - **Metric to Metric Conversions**

Surface Area and Temperature

Convert the following, as indicated:

68. 21,000 sq. meters = _____ ares   **69.** 16.5 hectares = _____ sq. meters

70. 2,690 ares = _____ hectares

71. 5,000 square meters = _____ hectares

72. 38.5° C = _____ degrees F

73. 302° F = _____ degrees C

74. What metric units would you use to measure each of the following:
   A. The weight of a person?   **B.** The distance between two cities?

   C. The height of a building?   **D.** The capacity of an automobile gas tank?

   E. The size of a farm?   **F.** The height of a person?

   G. Amount of medicine in a pill?   **H.** The diameter of the face of a wrist watch?

Check your answers with the correct answers and worked-out solutions in the appendix

Metric to U. S. and U. S. to Metric Conversions

The following alphabetical conversion table can be used to convert the most common U. S. and metric units. Note that the math procedure for each conversion is multiplication. Remember, don't try to memorize the conversion factors; learn to "use" the conversion tables as your tools! In everyday business, the more frequently you use various measurements, both U. S. and metric, the more familiar they will become.

Conversion Table - Metric to U. S. and U. S. to Metric

To convert from	To	Multiply
Acre	hectares	acres by .4047
Ares	sq. yards	ares by 119.6
Bushels	liters	bushels by 35.238
Centimeters	inches	centimeters by 0.3937
Centimeters	yards	centimeters by 0.01094
Cubic centimeters	cu. inches	cubic centimeters by 0.061
Cubic inches	cu. centimeters	cubic inches by 16.3872
Cubic inches	liters	cubic inches by 0.0164
Cubic yards	cu. meters	cubic yards by 0.7656
Feet	meters	feet by 0.3048
Gallons	liters	gallons by 3.7854
Grams	ounces	grams by 0.0353
Hectare	acres	hectares by 2.471
Inches	centimeters	inches by 2.54
Kilograms	pounds	kilograms by 2.2046
Kilograms	tons	kilograms by 0.0011
Kilometers	miles	kilometers by 0.6214
Liters	cu. inches	liters by 61.025
Liters	gallons	liters by 0.2642
Liters	quarts (dry)	liters by 0.9081
Liters	ounces (fluid)	liters by 33.7838
Liters	quarts (fluid)	liters by 1.0567
Meters	feet	meters by 3.2808
Meters	inches	meters by 39.370
Meters	yards	meters by 1.094
Miles	kilometers	miles by 1.6093
Ounces (dry)	grams	ounces by 28.35
Ounces (fluid)	liters	ounces by 0.0296
Pecks	liters	pecks by 8.8096

To convert from	To	Multiply
Pint (dry)	cu. centimeters	pints by 550.41
Pint (fluid)	cu. centimeters	pints by 473.179
Pounds	kilograms	pounds by 0.4536
Quarts (dry)	cu. centimeters	quarts by 1101.23
Quarts (fluid)	liters	quarts by 0.9463
Square centimeters	sq. inches	sq. centimeters by 0.155
Square feet	sq. meters	sq. feet by 0.0929
Square inches	sq. centimeters	sq. inches by 6.4517
Square meters	sq. inches	sq. meters by 1550.0
Square meters	sq. feet	sq. meters by 10.764
Square meters	sq. yards	sq. meters by 1.196
Square yards	sq. meters	sq. yards by 0.836
Tons (short)	kilograms	tons by 907.1846
Tons (short)	tons (metric)	tons (short) by 0.9072
Tons (metric)	tons (short)	tons (metric) by 1.1023
Yards	meters	yards by 0.9144

TRY-IT EXERCISES U. S. to Metric and Metric to U. S.

75. Joe is 69 inches tall and his wife Alice is 63½ inches tall.

A. What are their heights in feet and inches?

B. If an international passport application asked for their heights in meters, what are Joe and Alice's metric heights?

76. For a party, you estimate that each guest will drink 18 oz. of soda. If 22 guests are expected, how many 1-liter bottles of soda should you purchase?

77. You are the shipping manager of a factory that makes custom electric motors for export to Europe. If your Model 21 motor weighs 160 lbs., and the shipping crate weighs 22 lbs., 8 oz.,

    A. What is the total weight of a shipment of 7 motors?

    B. What is the equivalent weight of the motors in the metric system?

    C. If the freight charges are quoted as $.63 per kilogram, what is the total cost to ship the motors?

78. If a truck is traveling at a speed of 66 kilometers per hour, how many miles will it travel in 45 minutes.

79. For weeks you have been thinking about refinishing your backyard deck, and today is the day! The deck measures 24 feet by 9 feet. When you get to the store you read the label on the can, which states that each can covers 9 square meters of decking. If you want to put on two coats, how many cans will be required for the project?

Check your answers with the correct answers and worked-out solutions in the appendix.

Student Notes

Section IV
Assessment Test

(Use the Answer Sheet provided at the end of this test.)

1. In the giftwrap department of a retail store it is estimated that, on the average, a package requires 2 ft. 9 in. of cellophane tape. During the holiday season, the department wraps 215 packages per day, 7 days per week, for 8 weeks. As purchasing manager for the store, how many 300 yd. rolls of tape should you order to cover the expected volume in that department?

2. You are the warehouse manager for the Rand Corporation. An order of merchandise has just arrived in boxes 14½ in. high. If the warehouse has a 13 ft. ceiling,
   A. How many boxes can be stacked together?

   B. How many inches clearance to the ceiling will still be left?

3. A storage area is 15 ft., 5 in. by 22 ft., 8 in. If boxes 18 inches square containing electronic equipment can only be stacked 5 high,
   A. What is the maximum number of boxes that can be stored in this warehouse?

   B. If the storage charge is $.15 per day, per box, what is the monthly rental charge for July?

4. You are the shipping manager for a toy manufacturer that makes jigsaw puzzles. Each puzzle weighs 12 oz.; each box containing the puzzle weighs 6¼ oz.; and each shipping carton, which holds 48 boxes of puzzles, weighs 3½ lb.,

   A. How much does each loaded shipping carton weigh?

   B. If an order for 1,152 puzzles was received from a large chain of toy stores in Toledo, and the shipping charges from your plant to the customer are $.22 per pound, what is the total cost to ship the puzzles?

   C. If insurance on the order amounted to $4.90 per hundredweight, how much will it cost to insure the shipment?

   D. If another freight company quoted you $.18 per pound for shipping, and $5.70 per hundredweight for insurance, how much can be saved by choosing the lower price?

5. A production machine can make a plastic part every 90 seconds. If the factory has 11 of these machines,

   A. How many can be produced in an 8-hour shift?

   B. If your company purchases 5 additional machines, which are a faster model and can produce a part every 72 seconds, what is the total hourly production from the entire department?

6. Your branch office in Germany has just purchased merchandise from a company in Fort Worth, Texas. The amount of the order comes to $165,000. How many Deutsche marks will it take to pay for the merchandise?

7. A Japanese department store orders fine china from England. The total amount of the order comes to £8,000.
   A. How many yen will it take to pay for the china?

   B. If the same order was sent from England to Macy's in New York City, how many dollars would it amount to?

8. A food manufacturing process uses 5.7 grams of blended herbs and spices per package of gourmet frozen vegetables. How many packages can be produced from an 11.4 kilogram container of spices?

9. If Willie the weatherman says it was 86° Fahrenheit today,
   A. What is the corresponding temperature on the Celsius scale?

   B. If Willie's forecast for tonight is 20° Celsius, what temperature is that on the Fahrenheit scale?

10. You have a 5½ gallon plastic gasoline can for your lawnmower. When you fill the can at the corner gas station you find that the gasoline is priced at $.78 per liter.

    A. How many liters of gas will it take to fill the can?

    B. What will be the cost to fill the can?

11. The All-City Paving Company estimates that its crew can pave 35 meters per hour of highway with new asphalt.

    A. How many total hours will it take to pave 6½ miles of highway? (Round to the nearest whole hour.)

    B. How many 5¼ hour work days will be required to complete the job? (Round to the nearest whole day.)

    C. The crew consists of 4 experienced workers earning $14 per hour; 3 apprentice helpers earning $8.80 per hour; and a crew chief earning $17.50 per hour. How much is the crew labor expense for the entire 6½ mile highway job?

12. You are a real estate salesperson. One of your listed properties is a large undeveloped lot measuring 200 feet long by 436.5 feet wide.

    A. How many acres is this property?

B. If the asking price is $435,000, what is the price per acre?

C. If a German client asked you, "How many ares is this property," what would be your answer?

D. If he offered $51 per square meter, what was his total offer?

13. Kelloggs markets its products worldwide. What would be the metric weight in grams for the following cereal packages: (Round to the nearest whole gram.)
    A. 12 ounces - Corn Flakes?

    B. 1 pound, 3 ounces - Frosted Flakes?

    C. 2¼ pound - Sugar Smacks?

    D. What is the weight in kilograms of a gross, 12 dozen, boxes of Frosted Flakes?

14. An American tourist in Hong Kong wants to have some shirts tailor made. If his neck size is 16¼ inches, and the sleeve size 34½ inches, what measurements in centimeters should the tailor use? (Round to the nearest tenth.)

15. Martin Cornell's strawberry farm in England produces 850 kilograms of strawberries per hectare, per season. If the farm is 12½ hectares and there are 3 growing seasons per year, how many pounds of strawberries are produced each year on the farm? (Round to the nearest whole pound.)

16. The speed limit in your neighborhood is 40 miles per hour. (Round to nearest kilometer per hour.)
    A. What is the equivalent speed in kilometers per hour?

    B. The "school zone" speed limit is 15 MPH, what is the equivalent speed in kilometers per hour?

17. While on vacation in Europe you felt a bit ill, so you purchased a thermometer and took your temperature. If the reading on the thermometer was 37° C, what was your temperature in degrees F?

18. The distance between Pleasantville and Surfside is 322 kilometers. If a salesman had an appointment in Surfside at 3:00 PM, what is the latest time he can leave Pleasantville and still be on time, traveling at 50 miles per hour?

19. An automobile mechanic finds that since many engines are now built on the metric system, he needs to buy a set of metric wrenches. What are the metric equivalents in millimeters for the following: (Round to the nearest whole millimeter)

A. 1/2" wrench?

B. 3/4" wrench?

C. 1 1/4" wrench?

BUSINESS DECISION:
"The International Order"

20. You are the shipping manager for World Exports, Inc. You have just received an order for 5,000 am/fm radios from an importer who wants 3,000 sent to their warehouse in Berlin and billed in German marks; 1,300 sent to their London location, and billed in pounds; and the balance sent to Japan and billed in Yen. Each radio sells for $45.00 plus the following shipping and handling charges:

    Germany - $1.50 each   Britain - $1.15 each   Japan -$3.05 each

    A. Calculate the subtotals and total order in U.S. dollars.

    B. Convert the German portion to marks.

    C. Convert the British portion to pounds.

    D. Convert the Japanese portion to Yen.

Course_____   Name _____
Term:_____   St#_____
Professor_____   Date:_____

A Little Math With Your Business
Assessment Test - Section IV
Answer Sheet

1.	_____	12C.	_____
2A.	_____	12D.	_____
2B.	_____	13A.	_____
3A.	_____	13B.	_____
3B.	_____	13C.	_____
4A.	_____	13D.	_____
4B.	_____	14.	Neck _____
4C.	_____		Sleeve _____
4D.	_____	15.	_____
5A.	_____	16A.	_____
5B.	_____	16B.	_____
6.	_____	17.	_____
7A.	_____	18.	_____
7B.	_____	19A.	_____
8.	_____	19B.	_____
9A.	_____	19C.	_____
9B.	_____	20A.	_____
10A.	_____	20B.	_____
10B.	_____	20C.	_____
11A.	_____	20D.	_____
11B.	_____		
11C.	_____		
12A.	_____		
12B.	_____		

APPENDIX

ANSWERS

ASSESSMENT EXERCISE #1
Whole Numbers

$$\boxed{\textbf{ANSWERS}}$$

1. 200,049   Two hundred thousand, forty-nine.

2. 12,308,411   Twelve million, three hundred eighty thousand, four hundred eleven.

3. 316,229

4. 4,560,000

5. 18,300

6. 4,000,000

7. 260,000

8. 2,362,115

9. 77,597

10. 1,689,688

11. 17

12.

	Monday	Tuesday	Wednesday	Thursday	Friday	Saturday	Total Units
Records	82	56	68	57	72	92	427
Tapes	29	69	61	58	82	75	374
CDs	96	103	71	108	112	159	649
Daily Totals	207	228	200	223	266	326	1,450

13. $14,524

14. $1,003

15. $119,770

16. $520

17A. $11,340

17B. $36

  18. $2,825

19A. $4,975

19B. $1,990

  20. $4,500

ASSESSMENT EXERCISE #2
Fractions

$$\boxed{\textbf{ANSWERS}}$$

1. Improper fraction   Eighteen elevenths

2. Mixed number   Four and one-sixth

3. Proper fraction   Thirteen-sixteenths

4. $6\frac{1}{3}$

5. 25

6. $5\frac{1}{4}$

7. $\frac{86}{9}$

8. $\frac{8}{9}$

9. $\frac{2}{5}$

10. $\frac{20}{25}$

11. $\frac{18}{78}$

12. 60

13. $\frac{25}{36}$

14. $1\frac{3}{4}$

15. $5\frac{1}{3}$

16. $\frac{5}{24}$

17. $69

18. $6\frac{5}{8}$

19. $33

20A.   612

20B.   13,464

21A.   22⅜

21B. $223,750

22A.   184 oz.

22B.   11½ lb.

  23. $17,125

24A. $180

24B. $132

  25.   15 oz. Pasta

       3⅛ cup Tomatoes

       5 Tbs. Cheese

ASSESSMENT EXERCISE #3
Decimals

ANSWERS

1. Six hundred two, ten thousandths

2. Thirty-four, and four hundred eighty-one thousandths

3. One hundred nineteen dollars and eighty-five cents

4. .0967

5. 5.014

6. 6,843.15

7. $16.57

8. .45

9. 995.1

10. $128

11. $4.25

12. 51.071

13. $37.19

14. 473.824

15. 7.7056

16. $92.83

17. .837

18. 221.1

19. .156

20. 99,120

21. 17.3

22. .07904

23. $20.06

24. $1,127.85

25. $75.15

26. $1,500.36

27A. $2,640

27B. $200

28. $21,773.77

29. No! Overweight by 657.8 lbs.

30A. $7.25

30B. $426.25

SECTION II

TRY-IT EXERCISES

ANSWERS

1. .27

2. 4.72

3. .937

4. .0081

5. .1275

6. .00875

7. 80%

8. 140%

9. .23%

10. 1.64%

11. 1900%

12. 57.67%

13. 539

14. 2,415

15. 200

16. $22,275

17. 40.9%

18. 47.2%

19. 30%

20. 62.4%

21. 1,725

22. $620

23. 160

24. 4,000

25. 45.8%

26. 28.6%

27. 17.8%

28. 78.2%

29. 208

30. 520

31. 66.7

32. 20 feet

33. 40%

SECTION III

TRY-IT EXERCISES

1. 454.2 people per seminar

2A. Median = 48   Range = 89

2B. Median = 4,237   Range = 5,338

3. Mode = 10

4. Mean of grouped data = 50.67

See frequency distribution in Worked-Out Solutions on p. 137.

SECTION IV

TRY-IT EXERCISES

ANSWERS

LENGTH
1. 35 yd.
2. 13 ft.
3. 12,672 ft.
4. 102 in.
5. 12 yd.
6. 33 ft.
7. 4½ or 4.5 mi.
8. 117 in.
9. 6.6 miles
10. 3,727 paces

SURFACE AREA
11. 3¾ or 3.75 sq. ft.
12. 246,840 sq. yd.
13. 8,820 sq. ft.
14. 127 sq. miles
15. 2.2 acres
16. 34,560 sq. ft.
17. 1,600 acres
18. 86 sq. yd.
19. 8.9 sq. miles
20A. 270 sq. feet
20B. 30 yd.
20C. $959.00 total cost

VOLUME, LIQUID & DRY
21. 5 pints
22. 96 qts.
23. 189 cu. ft.
24. 7½ or 7.5 cu. ft.
25. 6⅜ or 6.375 pecks
26. 78.4 qts.
27. 16¾ or 16.75 qts.
28. 164 pecks
29A. 796.25 gallons
29B. $2,452.45 total cost
30. $31.16

WEIGHT
31. 2¼ or 2.25 lbs.
32. 224 oz.
33. 8,400 lbs.
34. 22 tons (long)
35. 41 lbs.
36. 2,040 oz.
37. 1.7 tons (short)
38. 12 oz.
39. 168 lbs. 4 oz.
40A. Yes
40B. Safe by 2,150 lbs.

TIME
41. 1½ or 1.5 days
42. 150 sec.
43. 9 weeks
44. 75 min.
45. 2½ or 2.5 hours
46. 3½ or 3.5 min.
47. 84 days
48. 2¾ or 2.75 years
49A. 5½ or 5.5 years
49B. Start 1993 – last pmt – Sept. 1, 1998
Start 1994 – last pmt – Sept. 1, 1999
Start 1995 – last pmt – Sept. 1, 2000
Start 1996 – last pmt – Sept. 1, 2001
50. $158.10

CURRENCY CONVERSION
51. £232.38
52. 236.44 DM
53. ¥1,024,065
54. $195.36
55A. £968.25
55B. $207.55

METRIC TO METRIC
Length, Volume, Weight
56. .32 m.
57. 5.7 cm.
58. 38,000 m.
59. 50,700 cm
60. 12,500 g.
61. 9,000 mg.
62. 24,000 dg.
63. 6,710 ml.
64. 5.69 l.
65. .383 l.
66. 1.8 kg.
67. 1.48 m.

METRIC TO METRIC
Surface area and temperature
68. 210 ares
69. 165,000 sq. meters
70. 269 hectares
71. ½ or .5 hectare
72. 101.3° F
73. 150° C

74A. Kilograms
74B. Kilometers
74C. Meters
74D. Liters
74E. Hectares or Square Meters
74F. Centimeters or Meters
74G. Milligrams
74H. Millimeters

U.S. to METRIC — METRIC to U.S.
75A. Joe: 5 ft. 9 in.
       Alice: 5 ft. 3½ in.
75B. Joe: 1.7526 meters
       Alice: 1.6129 meters
  76. 12 one liter bottles
77A. 1,142 lb. 8 oz.
77B. 518.2 kg.
77C. $326.47
  78. 30¾ or 30.75 miles
  79. 4½ or 4.5 cans

WORKED-OUT SOLUTIONS

WORKED-OUT SOLUTIONS TO WORD PROBLEMS
ASSESSMENT EXERCISE #1
Whole Numbers

13. Records $427 × 9 =   3,843
         Tapes   374 × 6 =   2,244
         CD's   649 × 13 = __8,437__
                                   $14,524 = Total

14. Starting balance   868
         Less – Total checks   −536
         Plus – Total deposits   __+671__
                                   $1,003 Ending balance

15. Actual profits   3,009,770
         Less projected profits   __−2,890,000__
                                   $ 119,770 Protection under actual.

16.   300 Commission   27,040 Yearly total
         ×   12 Months   ──────────────────── = $520 per week
              3,600 Yearly commission   52   Week/year
         __+23,440__ Yearly salary
         $27,040 Yearly total

17A. Cost of luncheon
              315 Persons
         ×   13 Cost per person
              4,095 Total cost – meals
           +2,100 Entertainment
           + 880 Facility rental
           +2,636 Printing
          __+1,629__ Other expenses
         $11,340 Total cost

17B. 11,340 Total cost
         ──────────────── = $36 Cost per person
           315 Persons

18. $ 565 Monthly payment
         ×   5 Bank requirement
         $2,825 Monthly income required to qualify for mortgage loan

19A. $165,000 Purchase price   119,400 Total loan
      − 45,600 Down payment   24   Months
      $119,400 Amount of loan   = $4,975 Monthly payment 2 years

19B. $\frac{\$119,400 \text{ Total loan}}{60 \quad \text{Months}}$ = $1,990 Monthly payment 5 years

20.   Star-Bright Security

Revenue
        30 Guards
×   25 Hours
        750 Total hours
×   14 Charge per hour
    $10,500 Total weekly revenue

Expenses
        30 Guards
×   25 Hours
        750 Total hours
×   8 Cost per hour
    $6,000 Total weekly expense

    $10,500 Revenue
    − 6,000 Expenses
    $ 4,500 Profit

WORKED-OUT SOLUTIONS TO WORD PROBLEMS
ASSESSMENT EXERCISE #2
Fractions

17. $\$161 \times \frac{3}{7} = \frac{483}{7} = \underline{\$69}$ earned Thursday

18. $6\frac{1}{8} + 7\frac{3}{4} + 4\frac{1}{2} = 18\frac{3}{8}$ hours worked
$25 - 18\frac{3}{8} = \underline{6\frac{5}{8}}$ hours left

19. $\$825 \times \frac{1}{25} = \underline{\$33}$ deducted

20A. $255 \div \frac{5}{12} = \underline{612}$ cans

20B.

Cans per container		Containers per hour		hours	
612	$\times$	$2\frac{3}{4}$	$\times$	8	$= \underline{13,464}$ cans in 8 hours

21A.
$3 \text{ lots} \times 1\frac{2}{3} \text{ acres} = 5 \text{ acres}$
$4 \text{ lots} \times 3\frac{3}{4} \text{ acres} = 15 \text{ acres}$
$1 \text{ lot} \times 2\frac{3}{8} \text{ acres} = \underline{2\frac{3}{8}} \text{ acres}$
$ \underline{22\frac{3}{8}} \text{ total acres}$

21B.

Total acres		Cost per acre		total cost
$22\frac{3}{8}$	$\times$	10,000	$=$	$\underline{\$223,750}$

22. Savings per jar = $11\frac{2}{3} - 7\frac{5}{6} = 3\frac{5}{6}$ ounces.
a. $3\frac{5}{6} \times 48 = \underline{184}$ ounces per carton

b. $\frac{184}{16} = \underline{11\frac{1}{2}}$ pounds per carton

23. $113\frac{7}{8} - 96\frac{3}{4} = \$17\frac{1}{8}$ profit per share
$17\frac{1}{8} \times 1,000 = \underline{\$17,125}$ profit

24A. $\$240 \times \frac{1}{4} = \$60$ discount
$240 - 60 = \underline{\$180}$ sale price

24B. $\$240 \times \frac{1}{5} = \$48$ additional discount-scratched model
$180 - 48 = \underline{\$132}$ sale price scratched

25.   For 5 people, multiply each quantity by $\frac{5}{8}$

Linguini = $24 \times \frac{5}{8} = \underline{15}$ ounces

Tomatoes = $5 \times \frac{5}{8} = \underline{\underline{3\frac{1}{8}}}$ cups

Cheese = $8 \times \frac{5}{8} = \underline{5}$ tablespoons

WORKED-OUT SOLUTIONS TO WORD PROBLEMS
ASSESSMENT EXERCISE #3
Decimals

24. $ 335.79 tuner
+ 435.67 amplifier
+ 287.99 CD player
+   23.76 CD's (2 × 11.88)
+   44.64 CD's (3 × 14.88)
$1,127.85 total cost

25. $315.10 original price
−239.95 sale price
$ 75.15 savings

26.

	Earnings per hour		hours		
Joe:	$17.75	×	43.22 =	767.16	
Gloria:	$19.50	×	37.6 =	733.20	
				$1,500.36 total earnings	

27A. Price   Pages   Quantity
$.066 ×   4   × 10,000 = $2,640 Cost: Great Impressions

27B. Price   Pages   Quantity
$.061 ×   4   × 10,000 = $2,440 Cost: Payless

$2,640 Great Impressions
−2,440 Payless
$ 200 savings

28. $ 546.11 monthly payment
×   24 months
$13,106.64 amount paid

  34,880.41 amount owed
−13,106.64 amount paid
$21,773.77 remaining

29.

	Quantity		Weight		
Plywood	145	×	18.6	=	2,697.0 pounds
Concrete	64	×	69.7	=	4,460.8 pounds
					7,157.8 Total weight

7,157.8 Total weight
−6,500.0 Truck capacity
   657.8 Overweight amount

Order <u>CANNOT</u> be shipped in 1 truckload.

30A. $137.80 plants
       7.95 soil (3 × 2.65)
     253.00 pots (55 × 4.60)
   $398.75 total cost

$$\frac{398.75}{55} = \underline{\$7.25} \text{ cost per plant}$$

30B. $ 15.00 selling price
   −   7.25 cost
   $ 7.75 profit per plant
   ×   55
   $426.25 profit

WORKED-OUT SOLUTIONS
TRY-IT EXERCISES
SECTION II

1-6.   Move decimal point two places left and remove percent sign.

1. $27\% = \underline{.27}$

2. $472\% = \underline{4.72}$

3. $93.7\% = \underline{.937}$

4. $.81\% = \underline{.0081}$

5. $12\frac{3}{4}\% = 12.75\% = \underline{.1275}$

6. $\frac{7}{8}\% = .875\% = \underline{.00875}$

7-12.   Move decimal point two places right and add percent sign.

7. $.8 = \underline{80\%}$

8. $1.4 = \underline{140\%}$

9. $.0023 = \underline{.23\%}$

10. $.016\frac{2}{5} = .0164 = \underline{1.64\%}$

11. $19 = \underline{1900\%}$

12. $.57\frac{2}{3} = .5767 = \underline{57.67\%}$

13. $P = R \times B$
$P = .55 \times 980$
$P = \underline{539}$

14. $P = R \times B$
$P = .75 \times 3,220$
$P = \underline{2,415}$

15. $P = R \times B$
$P = .16 \times 1250$
$P = \underline{200}$ employees in sales

16. $P = R \times B$
$P = .15 \times 148,500$
$P = \underline{\$22,275}$ down payment

17. $R = \dfrac{P}{B}$

$R = \dfrac{9}{22}$

$R = .409 = \underline{40.9\%}$

18. $R = \dfrac{P}{B}$

$R = \dfrac{67}{142}$

$R = .4718 = \underline{47.2\%}$

19. $R = \dfrac{P}{B}$

$R = \dfrac{5,400}{18,000}$

$R = .3 = \underline{30\%}$ completed

20. $R = \dfrac{P}{B}$

$R = \dfrac{5,600}{8,970}$

$R = .6243 = \underline{62.4\%}$ suits

21. $B = \dfrac{P}{R}$

$B = \dfrac{690}{.4}$

$B = \underline{1,725}$

22. $B = \dfrac{P}{R}$

$B = \dfrac{545.60}{.88}$

$B = \underline{620}$

23. $B = \dfrac{P}{R}$

$B = \dfrac{120}{.75}$

$B = \underline{160}$ motors

24. $B = \dfrac{P}{R}$

$B = \dfrac{3400}{.85}$

$B = \underline{4,000}$ reams

25. $R = \dfrac{P}{B}$ (P = amount of increase) (B = original amount)

$R = \dfrac{948 - 650}{650}$

$R = .4584 = \underline{45.8\%}$ Increase

26. $R = \dfrac{P}{B}$ (P = amount of decrease) (B = original amount)

$R = \dfrac{21 - 15}{21}$

$R = .2857 = \underline{28.6\%}$ decrease

27. $R = \dfrac{P}{B}$ (P = salary increase) (B = original salary)

$R = \dfrac{530 - 450}{450}$

$R = .1777 = \underline{17.8\%}$ Increase

28. $R = \dfrac{P}{B}$ (P = decrease in defects) (B = original number of defects)

$R = \dfrac{55 - 12}{55}$

$R = .7818 = \underline{78.2\%}$ Decrease

29. $P = R \times B$ (R = 100% + 30%) (B = original number of megabytes)

$P = 1.3 \times 160$
$P = \underline{208}$ megabytes

30. $P = R \times B$ (R = 100% − 20%) (B = original number of miles)

$P = .8 \times 650$
$P = \underline{520}$ miles

31. $B = \dfrac{P}{R}$ (P = new amount of acres)
       (R = 100% + 20%)

   $B = \dfrac{80}{1.2}$

   $B = .6666 = \underline{66.7}$ acres

32. $B = \dfrac{P}{R}$ (P = new water level)
       (R = 100% − 40%)

   $B = \dfrac{12}{.6}$

   $B = \underline{20}$ feet

33. $R = \dfrac{\text{Change in percentage points}}{\text{Original percentage points}}$

   $R = \dfrac{8}{20}$

   $R = .4 = \underline{40\%}$ Increase

WORKED-OUT SOLUTIONS
TRY-IT EXERCISES
SECTION III

1. Arithmetic mean = $\dfrac{\text{sum of values}}{\text{number of values}}$

$$\frac{433 + 247 + 661 + 418 + 512}{5} = \frac{2271}{5} = \underline{454.2} \text{ mean}$$

2A. Arrange data in rank order:

12 13 29 33 42 54 76 79 81 101

Median
Since number of values is even (10), median is midway between the 5th & 6th values.

$$\frac{42 + 54}{2} = \frac{96}{2} = \underline{48} \text{ Median}$$

Range
Difference between lowest and highest value
101 − 12 = $\underline{89}$ Range

2B. Arrange data in rank order:

1220 2430 3619 4237 4589 5840 6558

Median
Since number of values is odd (7), median is the middle value.
Median = $\underline{4237}$

Range
Difference between lowest and highest value
6558 − 1220 = $\underline{5338}$ Range

3. Mode is the value occurring most frequently.

Value	Frequency
10	7
20	5
55	3
65	1
85	1
125	1

Mode = <u>10</u>

4.

Class	Tally	Freq (f)	Midpoint (m)	f × m
10 – 20	IIII	4	15	60
20 – 30	IIII	4	25	100
30 – 40	III	3	35	105
40 – 50	IIII	4	45	180
50 – 60	III	3	55	165
60 – 70	III	3	65	195
70 – 80	IIII I	6	75	450
80 – 90	II	2	85	170
90 – 100	I	1	95	95
		30		1,520

$$\text{Mean} = \frac{\text{sum of f} \times \text{m}}{\text{number of sum of f}} = \frac{1,520}{30} = \underline{50.7}$$

WORKED-OUT SOLUTIONS
TRY-IT EXERCISES
SECTION IV

1. $\text{Yards} = \dfrac{\text{feet}}{3} = \dfrac{105}{3} = \underline{\underline{35}} \text{ yards}$

2. $\text{Feet} = \dfrac{\text{inches}}{12} = \dfrac{156}{12} = \underline{\underline{13}} \text{ feet}$

3. $\text{Feet} = \text{miles} \times 5{,}280$
    $2.4 \times 5{,}280 = \underline{\underline{12{,}672}} \text{ feet}$

4. $\text{Inches} = \text{feet} \times 12$
    $8\frac{1}{2} \times 12 = \underline{\underline{102}} \text{ inches}$

5. $\text{Yards} = \dfrac{\text{inches}}{36} = \dfrac{432}{36} = \underline{\underline{12}} \text{ yards}$

6. $\text{Feet} = \text{yards} \times 3$
    $11 \times 3 = \underline{\underline{33}} \text{ feet}$

7. $\text{Miles} = \dfrac{\text{feet}}{5{,}280} = \dfrac{23{,}760}{5{,}280} = \underline{\underline{4.5}} \text{ miles}$

8. $\text{Inches} = \text{yards} \times 36$
    $3\frac{1}{4} \times 36 = \underline{\underline{117}} \text{ inches}$

9. $\text{Miles} = \dfrac{\text{feet}}{5{,}280} = \dfrac{35{,}000}{5{,}280} = \underline{\underline{6.6}} \text{ miles}$

10. $\dfrac{\text{Feet per mile}}{\text{Feet per pace}} = \dfrac{5{,}280}{4.25} = 1{,}242.4 \text{ paces per mile}$

    $\text{Paces per mile} \times \text{miles} = \text{total paces}$
    $1{,}242.4 \times 3 = \underline{\underline{3{,}727}} \text{ paces}$

11. $\text{Sq. feet} = \dfrac{\text{sq. inches}}{144} = \dfrac{540}{144} = \underline{3.75}$ sq. feet

12. Sq. yards = acres × 4,840
     $51 \times 4{,}840 = \underline{246{,}840}$ sq. yards

13. Sq. feet = sq. yards × 9
     $980 \times 9 = \underline{8{,}820}$ sq. feet

14. $\text{Sq. miles} = \dfrac{\text{acres}}{640} = \dfrac{81280}{640} = \underline{127}$ sq. miles

15. $\text{Acres} = \dfrac{\text{sq. yards}}{4{,}840} = \dfrac{10{,}648}{4{,}840} = \underline{2.2}$ acres

16. Sq. inches = sq. feet × 144
     $240 \times 144 = \underline{34{,}560}$ sq. inches

17. Acres = sq. miles × 640
     $2.5 \times 640 = \underline{1{,}600}$ acres

18. $\text{Sq. yards} = \dfrac{\text{sq. feet}}{9} = \dfrac{774}{9} = \underline{86}$ sq. yards

19. $\text{Sq. miles} = \dfrac{\text{acres}}{640} = \dfrac{5{,}696}{640} = \underline{8.9}$ sq. miles

20A. Area = length × width
     $15 \times 18 = \underline{270}$ sq. feet

20B. $\text{Sq. yards} = \dfrac{\text{sq. feet}}{9} = \dfrac{270}{9} = \underline{30}$ sq. yards

20C. **Carpet** sq. yards × price
     $30 \times 18.55 = \$556.50$ carpet
     Padding sq. feet × price
     $270 \times .75 = \$202.50$ padding
     Labor   Flat Fee = $\underline{\$200.00}$ labor
                               $\underline{\$959.00}$ total cost

21. $\text{Pints} = \dfrac{\text{fl. ounces}}{16} = \dfrac{80}{16} = \underline{5}$ pints

22. Quarts = pecks × 8
     $12 \times 8 = \underline{96}$ quarts

23.   Cu. feet = cu. yards × 27

$$7 \times 27 = \underline{189} \text{ cu. feet}$$

24. $\text{Cu. feet} = \dfrac{\text{cu. inches}}{1,728} = \dfrac{12,960}{1,728} = \underline{7.5} \text{ cu. feet}$

25. $\text{Pecks} = \dfrac{\text{quarts}}{8} = \dfrac{51}{8} = \underline{6\frac{3}{8}} \text{ or } \underline{6.375} \text{ pecks}$

26.   Quarts = gallons × 4

$$19.6 \times 4 = \underline{78.4} \text{ quarts}$$

27. $\text{Quarts} = \dfrac{\text{pints}}{2} = \dfrac{33.5}{2} = \underline{16\frac{3}{4}} \text{ or } \underline{16.75} \text{ quarts}$

28.   Pecks = bushels × 4

$$41 \times 4 = \underline{164} \text{ pecks}$$

29A.

Oil/motor		Motors/shift		Shifts/day		Days/week		Weeks	
2.6	×	35	×	2	×	5	×	7	= 6,370 pints

$$\frac{6,370 \text{ pints}}{2} = \underline{3,185} \text{ quarts}$$

$$\frac{3,185 \text{ quarts}}{4} = \underline{796.25} \text{ gallons}$$

29B.   Quarts × price

3,185 × .77 = $\underline{\$2,452.45}$ cost of oil

30.

$$1 \text{ bushel} = 4 \text{ pecks}$$
$$4 \text{ pecks} \times 8 = 32 \text{ quarts}$$
$$32 \text{ quarts} \times 2 = 64 \text{ pints}$$
$$64 \times 1.19 = \$76.16 \text{ revenue}$$
$$\underline{-45.00} \text{ cost}$$
$$\underline{\$31.16} \text{ gross profit}$$

31. $\text{Pounds} = \dfrac{\text{ounces}}{16} = \dfrac{36}{16} = \underline{2.25} \text{ or } \underline{2\frac{1}{4}} \text{ pounds}$

32.   Ounces = pounds × 16

$$14 \times 16 = \underline{224} \text{ ounces}$$

33.   Pounds = tons (short) × 2,000

$$4.2 \times 2,000 = \underline{8,400} \text{ pounds}$$

34.   Tons (long) $= \dfrac{\text{pounds}}{2,240} = \dfrac{49,280}{2,240} = \underline{\underline{22}}$ tons (long)

35.   Pounds $= \dfrac{\text{ounces}}{16} = \dfrac{656}{16} = \underline{\underline{41}}$ pounds

36.   Ounces = pounds × 16
   $127.5 \times 16 = \underline{\underline{2,040}}$ ounces

37.   Tons (short) $= \dfrac{\text{pounds}}{2,000} = \dfrac{3,400}{2,000} = \underline{\underline{1.7}}$ tons (short)

38.   Ounces = pounds × 16
   $.75 \times 16 = \underline{\underline{12}}$ ounces

39.   Sam weighs $\dfrac{(88 \text{ ounces})}{16}$ = 5½ pounds less than John

   5½ pounds = 5 pounds 8 oz.
   John   173 lb   12 oz
        $-$ 5 lb   8 oz
   $\underline{\underline{168 \text{ lb}}}$ $\underline{\underline{4 \text{ oz}}}$ = Sam's weight

40A.   8.5 tons × 2,000 = 17,000 lb limit
   4,550 + 10,300 = 14,850 lb (truck + load)
   <u>Yes!</u> Safe to cross bridge.

40B.   17,000 load limit
   $-14,850$ load
    $\underline{\underline{2,150}}$ pound margin of safety

41.   Days $= \dfrac{\text{hours}}{24} = \dfrac{36}{24} = \underline{\underline{1.5}}$ or $\underline{\underline{1\frac{1}{2}}}$ days

42.   Seconds = minutes × 60
   $2.5 \times 60 = \underline{\underline{150}}$ seconds

43.   Weeks $= \dfrac{\text{days}}{7} = \dfrac{63}{7} = \underline{\underline{9}}$ weeks

44.   Minutes = hours × 60
   $1.25 \times 60 = \underline{\underline{75}}$ minutes

45.   Hours $= \dfrac{\text{minutes}}{60} = \dfrac{150}{60} = \underline{\underline{2.5}}$ or $\underline{\underline{2\frac{1}{2}}}$ hours

46. $\text{Minutes} = \dfrac{\text{seconds}}{60} = \dfrac{210}{60} = \underline{\underline{3.5}}$ or $\underline{\underline{3\frac{1}{2}}}$ minutes

47.   Days = weeks × 7

   $12 \ \times 7 = \underline{\underline{84}}$ days

48. $\text{Years} = \dfrac{\text{months}}{12} = \dfrac{33}{12} = \underline{\underline{2.75}}$ or $\underline{\underline{2\frac{3}{4}}}$ years

49A. $\dfrac{66 \text{ months}}{12} = \underline{\underline{5.5}}$ or $\underline{\underline{5\frac{1}{2}}}$ years

49B.

Current year	Final payment
1993	Sept. 1, 1998
1994	Sept. 1, 1999
1995	Sept. 1, 2000
1996	Sept. 1, 2001

50.   2:45 PM to 4:18 PM = 1 hour 33 minutes

   or 93 minutes

Min	Cost

   $93 \ \times 1.70 = \underline{\underline{\$158.10}}$ cost of simulator session

51.   Pounds = dollars × .64550

   $360 \ \times .64550 = \underline{\underline{232.38}}$ pounds

52.   Deutsche marks = yen × .01285

   $18,400 \times .01285 = \underline{\underline{236.44}}$ Deutsche marks

53.   Yen = pounds × 227.57

   $4,500 \ \times 227.57 = \underline{\underline{1,024,065}}$ yen

54.   Dollars = Deutsche marks × .65120

   $300 \times .65120 = \underline{\underline{195.36}}$ dollars

55A.   Pounds = dollars × .64550

   $1,500 \ \times .64550 = \underline{\underline{968.25}}$ pounds

55B.   Dollars = pounds × 1.5605

   $133 \ \times 1.5605 = \underline{\underline{207.55}}$ dollars

56.   32 cm = $\underline{\underline{.32}}$ m   **57.**   57 mm = $\underline{\underline{5.7}}$ cm

   2 places left   1 place left

58. 38 km = <u>38,000</u> m
3 places right

59. 507 m = <u>50,700</u> cm
2 places right

60. 12.5 kg = <u>12,500</u> g
3 places right

61. 9 g = <u>9000</u> mg
3 places right

62. 24 hg = <u>24,000</u> dg
3 places right

63. 6.7 l = <u>6,710</u> ml
3 places right

64. 569 cl = <u>5.69</u> l
2 places left

65. 383 ml = <u>.383</u> l
3 places left

66. 1,800 g = <u>1.8</u> kg
3 places left

67. 148 cm = <u>1.48</u> m
2 places left

68. $\text{Ares} = \dfrac{\text{sq. meters}}{100} = \dfrac{21,000}{100} = \underline{210}$ ares

69. Sq. meters = hectares × 10,000
$16.5 \times 10,000 = \underline{165,000}$ sq. meters

70. $\text{Hectares} = \dfrac{\text{ares}}{10} = \dfrac{2,690}{10} = \underline{269}$ hectares

71. $\text{Hectares} = \dfrac{\text{sq. meters}}{10,000} = \dfrac{5,000}{10,000} = \underline{.5}$ or $\underline{\tfrac{1}{2}}$ hectare

72. F = 1.8 C + 32
F = 1.8 (38.5) + 32
F = <u>101.3°</u>F

73. C = ⅝ (F − 32)
C = ⅝ (302 − 32)
C = <u>150°</u>C

74A. Kilograms

74B. Kilometers

74C. Meters

74D. Liters

74E. Hectares or
sq. meters

74F. Centimeters or
meters

74G. Milligrams

74H. Millimeters

75A. $\text{Joe} = \dfrac{69}{12} = \underline{5}$ ft $\underline{9}$ in

$\text{Alice} = \dfrac{63.5}{12} = \underline{5}$ ft $\underline{3\tfrac{1}{2}}$ in

75B. Joe inches × 2.54 = cm

             69 × 2.54 = 175.26 cm = <u>1.7526</u> meters

      Alice inches × 2.54 = cm

             63.5 × 2.54 = 161.29 cm = <u>1.6129</u> meters

76.

<u>Guests</u>		<u>Ounces/guest</u>	<u>total ounces</u>
22	×	18	= 396 ounces

<u>ounces × .0296</u>	<u>= liters</u>
396 × .0296	= 11.7 or <u>12</u> 1-liter bottles

77A.

<u>Motors</u>		<u>Pounds/motor</u>		<u>Weight of motors</u>
7	×	160	=	1,120

      1,120 + 22 lb 8 oz = <u>1,142</u> lb <u>8</u> oz

77B. <u>Pounds</u>   <u>.4536</u> = <u>Kilograms</u>

      1142.5 × .4536 = <u>518.2</u> kg

77C.

<u>Kilograms</u>		<u>Cost/kg</u>		<u>Freight charge</u>
518.2	×	.63	=	<u>$326.47</u>

78. <u>Kilometers/hour × .6214 = miles/hour</u>

          66   × .6214 = 41 miles/hour

        41 miles per hour

    <u>× .75 hours (45 minutes)</u>

    <u>30.75</u> or 30¾ miles in 45 minutes

79. Deck area = 24 × 9 = 216 sq. feet

                            <u>× 2 coats</u>

                          433 sq. feet

      sq. feet × .0929 = sq. meters

       433 × .0929 = 40.1 sq. meters

$$\frac{40.1 \text{ sq. meters}}{9 \text{ meters/can}} = \underline{\underline{4.5}} \text{ or } \underline{\underline{4\frac{1}{2}}} \text{ cans}$$

Glossary PLUS

A

Accounts payable Amounts that are due creditors. Found on the liability side of the balance sheet.

Accounts receivable Amounts owed by customers to businesses for goods or services received but not paid for.

Accumulated depreciation The total amount that an asset has depreciated to date.

Acid-test ratio The ratio of liquid assets to current liabilities. Also known as the quick assets ratio.

Accelerated cost recovery system (ACRS) A depreciation method used for federal income tax purposes, whereby businesses are permitted to write off the cost of assets more quickly than their useful life.

Actuary A statistician who determines risks and premiums for insurance companies.

Addend Any of a set of numbers added in an addition problem.

Adjustable rate mortgage (ARM) Mortgage loan with interest varying up and down, based on the prevailing rates over the period of the loan.

Amortization Table A schedule showing the principal and interest necessary to pay off a loan over a period of time.

Annual percentage rate (APR) Actual or effective annual rate of interest on a loan or installment purchase. Truth in Lending Act requires disclosure of APR to customer at the time of sale.

Annuity Equal payments of money over a period of time.

Annuity due Annuity in which payments are made or received at the beginning of each time period.

Arithmetic mean See average or mean.

Assessed value The value of a piece of real estate. It is used as the basis for computing property taxes.

Asset Something of value owned by a business such as equipment or buildings. Assets are listed on the asset side of the balance sheet.

Automatic teller machine (ATM) Machines placed in convenient locations that allow bank customers to make withdrawals, deposits, and other banking transactions.

Average In statistics, a value that typifies or is representative of a whole range of values. Also known as the arithmetic mean. It is computed by dividing the sum of the values by the number of values.

B

Balance sheet An important financial statement summarizing the assets, liabilities, and owner's equity of a firm at any given time.

Balloon payment A large repayment of the principal at the maturity of certain loans.

Bank discount A method of lending money whereby the interest is deducted from the principal leaving the borrower with the proceeds.

Bank statement A monthly summary of the activities in a checking account, including debits, credits, and beginning and ending balance.

Banker's rule A method for calculating simple interest that uses a 360-day year and the exact time of a loan.

Bar graph A visual representation of data by the length of horizontal bars or vertical columns, often illustrating an increase or decrease in magnitude.

Base One of the variables of the percentage calculation; it is the starting point or basis upon which something is compared. (Base = 100%)

bbl. Abbreviation for barrel.

Bearer The person or institution physically holding a financial instrument such as a bond.

Bond Long-term debt instrument issued by a company or government agency to raise money.

Book Value The current accounting value of an asset; calculated as the original cost less the accumulated depreciation of that asset.

Broker A person who acts as an agent for buyers and sellers of stocks, bonds, real estate, and other investments.

C

Cancellation A process of reducing; used to simplify multiplication and division of fractions.

Capital The owner's amount of money in a business; determined by total assets minus total liabilities. Also known as owner's equity or net worth.

Capital gains Profits realized from investments such as real estate and stocks.

Cash discount Discount offered by sellers, over and above trade discounts, as an incentive for prompt payment of an invoice. For example, an extra 2% cash discount for paying within 10 days, rather than 30 days. Written – 2/10, net/30.

Celsius Temperature scale of the metric system, which registers the freezing point of water as 0°C, and the boiling point as 100°C.

Centi- A prefix used in the metric system meaning one hundredth of a basic unit. A centimeter, for example, is one hundredth of a meter.

Check A written order to a bank by a depositor to pay the amount specified on the check from funds on deposit in a checking account.

Circle graph A circle divided into sections representing the component parts of a whole in percentage terms. The whole, 100%, is the circle; the parts are the wedge-shaped sections of the circle.

Closing The final meeting in a real estate transaction in which the buyer, the seller, and the lender meet to sign documents and exchange monies.

COD Cash on delivery. Used in commerce when no credit terms have been established between buyer and seller.

Commission A fee charged by an agent for buyers and sellers of stocks, bonds, real estate and other investments. Usually expressed as a percent of the amount of the transaction.

Comparative graph A graph used to illustrate two or more related variables. May be in the form of a bar graph or line graph.

Comparative statements Statements illustrating data from two or more periods, with percentage change comparisons. The most common are the balance sheet and the income statement.

Compound interest The interest paid on principal and previously earned interest.

Cost Amount that a business pays to a manufacturer or supplier for merchandise. Also known as cost price.

Cost of goods sold The amount paid by a business for merchandise sold during an operating period.

cpm Abbreviation for cost per thousand. In advertising, for example, cpm represents the cost of an ad to reach one thousand people.

Current ratio An important accounting ratio; current assets divided by current liabilities. Used to indicate a company's short-term cash flexibility.

D

Deci- Prefix in the metric system meaning one tenth of a basic unit. For example, a deciliter is one tenth of a liter.

Decimal Any number written with a decimal point, such as 8.6 or .25. Also known as a decimal number.

Decimal equivalent A decimal having the same value as a fraction, such as: ¼ = .25

Decimal point A period placed to the left of a decimal number (.).

Deka- Prefix in the metric system meaning 10 times a basic unit. For example, a dekagram is 10 grams.

Deductions, Income tax Amounts that can be subtracted from gross earnings to determine taxable income. In business, all expenses are deductions; for individuals, some examples are mortgage interest, charitable contributions, and certain medical expenses.

Deductions, Payroll Amounts that are subtracted from an employee's gross earnings in order to arrive at net or take-home pay, such as federal income tax withholding, social security tax, and medicare tax.

Denominator The number of a fraction below the division line, such as 4 in the fraction ¾.

Depreciation The decline in market value of an asset over a period of time because of aging, usage, and obsolescence.

Difference The answer in a subtraction problem. For example, 4 is the difference of 6 minus 2.

Differential piece rate Method of compensating production employees whereby rate paid per unit increases as the number of units produced increases. For example, $2.30 per unit for the first 100 units, and $2.65 each over 100 units.

Digit Any one of the ten Arabic number symbols, 0 through 9, used in the decimal number system.

Discount, banking or finance To purchase or sell a bill, note, or other commercial paper, after deducting the amount of interest that will accumulate before maturity.

Discount, merchandising A reduction from the full or list price of an item.

Discount date The last date for a merchant to take advantage of a cash discount offered by a vendor.

Dividend The number being divided in a division problem. For example 15 is the dividend in the problem $15 \div 5 = 3$.

Dividend, finance A share of a company's profits distributed to the stockholders.

Divisor In division, the number doing the dividing. For example 5 is the divisor in the problem $15 \div 5 = 3$.

Draw An amount of money paid to a salesperson on commission as an advance against future commissions.

E

English system System of weights and measures primarily used in the United States. The fundamental units of this system are the yard and the pound. Also known as the U. S. Customary System.

Equation A mathematical statement using numbers, letters, and symbols to express a relationship of equality. $3X + 7 = 9$ is an equation.

Escrow account An account maintained by a lending institution that a mortgage borrower pays into to accumulate sufficient funds to pay property tax and insurance premiums when they are due.

Expenses The costs incurred by business in an attempt to sell goods and services. Divided into cost of merchandise and operating expenses.

Excise tax A tax levied by the federal government on the production, sale, or consumption of certain non-essential commodities such as tobacco, firearms, liquor, and other luxury items.

F

Face value The amount stated on the face of a promissory note or insurance policy. In finance, it is the amount borrowed. In insurance, it is the maximum amount for which the insurance company is responsible.

Fahrenheit Temperature scale of the U. S. Customary system, which registers the freezing point of water at 32°F, and the boiling point as 212°F.

Federal income tax withholding (FIT) Amount deducted from an employee's gross earnings each pay period as a contribution toward the federal income tax due for that year.

Federal Insurance Contributions Act (FICA) Amount deducted from an employee's gross earnings each pay period as a contribution toward Social Security and Medicare.

Federal Unemployment Tax Act (FUTA) Federal tax paid entirely by employers as funding toward federal and state unemployment programs.

Finance charge Total of installment payments for an item less the cost price of the item.

Floating decimal point A feature of most calculators that places the decimal point in the correct position in the final answer of a calculation.

Fraction An indicated quotient of two quantities. Expresses a portion of a whole. For example, the fraction ⅗ means 3 parts out of a total of 5 parts.

Frequency distribution In statistics, a table illustrating the number of times a certain event or value occurs within the classes of a set of grouped data.

G

Gram The basic unit of weight in the metric system. A gram is ¹⁄₂₈ of an ounce. A penny weighs about 2½ grams.

Greatest common divisor The largest number that divides evenly into the numerator and the denominator. Used to reduce a fraction to lowest terms.

Gross In commerce, a unit of measurement, twelve dozen, or 144 items.

Gross earnings The total amount of wages earned by an employee for a period of time before deductions.

Gross profit The total amount of revenue from the sale of goods and services less the cost of those goods and services.
Net sales − cost of goods sold.

Gross Sales Total amount of revenue from the sale of goods and services, before returns and allowances.

H

Hecto- Prefix of the metric system meaning 100 times a basic unit. For example, a hectometer is 100 meters.

Horizontal analysis A method of comparing data from two or more time periods. Illustrates the dollar amounts and percent change of the data between periods.

I

Improper fraction A fraction whose numerator is equal to or larger than the denominator. For example, ¼ and ⅘ are improper fractions. Improper fractions are used for intermediate calculations, but must be converted to whole or mixed numbers as a final answer.

Income Statement An important financial statement showing the revenues and expenses of a company over a period of time. Also known as an operating statement or profit and loss statement.

Individual retirement account (IRA) An investment account established by people to provide a retirement income in later years.

Integer Any number, 0 or greater, which does not contain a fraction or decimal. Also known as a whole number.
For example 4, 67, and 539 are integers.

Interest The charge assessed for borrowing money.
Interest = principal × rate × time.

Internal Revenue Service (IRS) Branch of the federal government that is responsible for collecting the income taxes due from business and individuals.

Inventory The amount in units or the value in dollars of the merchandise that a company has on hand to sell at any given time.

Inventory turnover A ratio indicating how many times the average inventory was sold during an operating period. Also known as stock turnover.
Inventory turnover = cost of goods sold ÷ average inventory at cost.

Invoice A document detailing a sales transaction, containing a list of goods shipped or services rendered, with an account of all costs.

K

Kilo- Prefix in the metric system meaning 1000 times a basic unit. For example, a kilometer is 1000 meters and a kilogram is 1000 grams.

L

Least common denominator The smallest whole number evenly divisible by the denominators of two or more fractions. For example, 6 is the least common denominator of ⅓ and ½.

Liability An amount owed to a creditor by a business. Liabilities are listed on the balance sheet.

Liquid assets Cash or other assets which can be readily converted to cash.

List price Suggested retail selling price of an item set by the manufacturer or supplier. The original price from which discounts are taken.

Line graph Graphical representation of data points on a grid connected by straight lines. Line graphs show change over a period of time.

Lowest terms A fraction reduced to a form in which only the number 1 can divide evenly into the numerator and the denominator. Lowest terms is the proper way to express an answer in fractions.

Liter Basic unit of volume in the metric system. A liter is slightly more than a quart.

M

Maker The person or institution that borrows money on a promissory note.

Markdown A reduction from the list price or original selling price of an item to promote sales. Markdowns may be expressed in dollars, or as percents "off" the list price.

Markup Amount added to the cost of an item to arrive at the selling price. Also known as gross profit or gross margin.
Markup = selling price − cost.

Markup based on cost When the amount of markup is calculated as a percent of the cost.
% Markup$_{cost}$ = amount of markup ÷ cost.

Markup based on selling price When the amount of markup is calculated as a percent of the selling price.
% Markup$_{s.p.}$ = amount of markup ÷ selling price.

Maturity value The total amount paid back on a loan by the borrower.
Maturity value = principal + interest.

Mean A numerical value that typifies, or is representative of, a whole range of values. Also known as the arithmetic mean. Corresponds to the generally accepted meaning of the word "average."
Arithmetic mean = sum of values ÷ number of values.

Median The midpoint value of a set of numbers when the numbers are ranked in ascending or descending order.

Memory function A feature found on most calculators today that stores numbers internally, allowing them to be recalled for calculation at a later time.

Merchant's Rule Method used to calculate the amount of credit given for the partial payment of a loan before the maturity date. See also United States Rule.

Meter Basic unit of length in the metric system. A meter is a little longer than a yard.

Metric system The standard international metric system of measurement, known as SI, is a decimal system, based on 10. The basic units are the meter for length, the liter for volume, and the gram for weight.

Mill A monetary unit equal to one tenth of a cent, or one thousandths of a dollar. (.001) Used in expressing and calculating property tax.

Milli- A prefix used in the metric system meaning thousandths of a basic unit. For example, a millimeter is one thousandths of a meter.

Minuend In a subtraction problem, the number from which another number is subtracted. For example, 25 is the minuend in the problem: $25 - 5 = 20$.

Mixed decimal A numerical value that is a combination of a whole number and a decimal number. For example, 45.057 is a mixed decimal.

Mixed number A numerical value combining a whole number and a fraction. For example, 12⅕, and 8¾ are mixed numbers.

Mode The value or values in a set of numbers which occur most often.

Mortgage A temporary pledge of property to a creditor as collateral against a debt. Used primarily in real estate.

Multiplicand The number that is to be multiplied by another number. For example, 20 is the multiplicand in the problem: $20 \times 2 = 40$.

Multiplier The number by which the multiplicand is multiplied. For example, 2 is the multiplier in the problem $20 \times 2 = 40$.

N

Net The remainder after all necessary deductions have been taken; as in net price, net weight, net profit, or net pay. Used in conjunction with "gross," meaning before deductions. Net amount = Gross amount – deductions.

Net income The difference between gross margin and operating expenses, as seen on the income statement. Also known as net earnings or net profit.

Net pay The amount of an employee's paycheck, after all deductions have been withheld. Also known as take-home pay.

Net price The cost or price of an item after trade discounts have been deducted. Also known as net cost.

Net proceeds Maturity value of a discounted note. The amount received from the bank after the discount amount is deducted from the amount of the loan. Also known as proceeds.

Net sales The amount of goods and services sold by a company after returns and allowances have been deducted. Net sales = gross sales – returns and allowances.

Net worth The difference between assets and liabilities. A balance sheet item. Also known as owner's equity or capital.

Noninterest-bearing note A promissory note where the maturity value is equal to the face value since there is no interest charged for borrowing the funds.

Nonsufficient funds (NSF) A situation in which a check is written without sufficient funds in the account to "cover" that check.

Numerator The number in a common fraction above the division line. For example, 7 is the numerator of the fraction $7/10$.

O

Operating expenses All expenses incurred in the operation of a business except the cost of the goods sold. An income statement item. Also known as overhead.

Ordinary annuity Annuity in which payments are made or received at the end of each time period.

Overhead All expenses incurred in the operation of a business except the cost of the goods sold. An income statement item. Also known as operating expenses.

Overtime Hours worked by employees over the usual 40 hours per week. Overtime hours are paid at a higher rate than regular time; frequently time and a half or double time.

Owner's equity The owner's amount of money in a business; determined by total assets minus total liabilities. A balance sheet item. Also known as capital or net worth.

P

Payee Person or institution named to receive the amount of a check.

Payer Person or institution named responsible for paying a bill or note.

Payroll register A spreadsheet record of the payroll data of a company for a period of time; including hours worked, rate per hour, payroll deductions, and net pay.

Percent Numerical term meaning "per hundred," or "parts per hundred," and is represented by the percent sign, %. Percents are numbers equal to a fraction with a denominator of 100. For example, five percent means 5 parts out of 100, and is written as 5 percent, 5%, 5 hundredths, $5/100$, or .05.

Percentage One of the variables of the percentage calculation. It is the number which represents a "part" or "portion" of the base. Percentage = rate × base.

Piecerate Method of compensating production workers whereby they receive a certain amount of pay per item produced or assembled.

Points A percent of the face value of a loan paid to the lender at closing as a fee for the preparation and administration of the loan. One point = one percent of the loan.

Premium The periodic amount of money charged by an insurance company for coverage by an insurance policy.

Present value Amount of money which must be deposited today in order to provide a specified lump sum of money in the future.

Present value of an annuity Amount of money which must be deposited today in order to provide a specified series of equal payments (annuity) in the future.

Price-earnings ratio (P/E) A ratio of the price of a share of stock divided by the earnings per share.

Prime number Number, larger than one, which is only divisible by one and itself. For example: 2, 3, 5, 7, 11, 13, 17, and 19 are prime numbers.

Principal A sum of money, either deposited or borrowed, upon which interest is calculated.
Principal = interest ÷ (rate × time).

Proceeds Maturity value of a discounted note. The amount received from the bank after the discount amount is deducted from the amount of a loan. Also known as net proceeds.

Product The answer of a multiplication problem. For example, 6 is the product of 2 × 3 = 6.

Promissory note A debt instrument in which one party agrees to repay money to another, within a specified amount of time, and at a specified rate of interest.

Proper fraction A fraction whose numerator is less than the denominator. For example, ⅚ is a proper fraction.

Property tax A tax levied by local governments on real estate and personal property to pay for education and other governmental services.

Prorate To distribute the amount of an expense over a period of time.

Q

Quick ratio An important accounting ratio of current assets less inventory to current liabilities.
Quick ratio = (current assets − inventory) ÷ current liabilities.

Quotient The answer of a division problem. For example, 8 is the quotient of 16 ÷ 2.

R

Rate One of the variables in the percentage calculations. Rate is always the variable with the percent (%) sign.
Rate = percentage ÷ base.

Ratio The relative size of two values expressed as the quotient of one divided by the other. For example, the ratio of 6 to 9 is written as ⁶⁄₉ or 6:9.

Reciprocals Numbers whose product is one. For example, the reciprocal of 5 is ⅕, since ⁵⁄₁ × ⅕ = 1.

Reconciling The process of comparing the checkbook records with the monthly bank statement.

Retained earnings Amount of earnings retained in the business for reinvestment in operations and expansion.

Return on investment (ROI) The percent representing the annual yield on an investment.
ROI = annual income ÷ amount of investment.

Revenue Amount of income realized by a firm, both cash and credit, from the sale of goods and services.

S

Salary A fixed amount of compensation for services paid to a person on a regular basis.

Sales tax State, county, or local government tax levied on sales of goods and services to the final consumer.

Selling price The price that the consumer pays for goods and services.

Selling price = cost + markup

Shift differential Extra wage incentive offered to employees for working undesirable hours, such as the midnight shift.

Simple interest Interest calculation which is computed solely on the principal amount borrowed.

Interest = principal × rate × time

Principal = interest ÷ (rate × time)

Rate = interest ÷ (principal × time)

Time = interest ÷ (principal × rate)

Sinking fund An annuity established to provide future funds for a specific purpose. Frequently used to systematically retire bonds or preferred stock of a corporation.

Stock turnover A ratio indicating how many times the average inventory was sold during an operating period. Also known as inventory turnover.

Stock turnover = cost of goods sold ÷ average inventory at cost.

Straight commission A method of salesperson's compensation whereby earnings are calculated as a percent of the value of goods and services sold.

Substitution Method used to verify the answer to an equation whereby the numerical solution is substituted back into the original equation each place the unknown variable appears. If the solution is indeed correct, the left and right sides of the equation will equal each other.

Subtrahend In a subtraction problem, the number which is being subtracted or taken from the minuend. For example, 5 is the subtrahend in the problem 25 − 5 = 20.

Sum The answer in an addition problem. For example, 7 is the sum in the problem 5 + 2 = 7.

Surface measure, Area Measure of two-dimensional objects, measured in square units, such as square yards or square meters. Area = length × width.

T

Terms of sale The portion of an invoice stating the cash discount percent and discount time period offered to purchaser as an incentive for early payment of the invoice. For example, an extra 3% cash discount for paying within 15 days, rather than the usual 45 days. Written - 3/15, net/45.

Time One of the variables of the simple interest formula, expressed in years.

Time = interest ÷ (principal × rate)

Trade discounts Reductions from the manufacturer's suggested list price, given to businesses for the performance of marketing functions such as selling, advertising, storage, service, and display. May be expressed as a single discount, such as 30%, or a series of discounts, such as 30%, 20%, written 30/20.

Truth in Lending Act Federal law requiring lenders to inform borrowers of the annual percentage rate and amount of finance charge on a loan, in writing.

U

United States Rule Generally accepted method of calculating the payoff of a loan before the maturity date; whereby payments are first credited to the interest due, and the balance used to reduce the principal

Unknowns The variables for which an equation is being solved, represented by letters of the alphabet or other symbols. For example, W represents the unknowns in the equation 4W − 5 = 21 + W.

Unlike fractions Proper fraction that have different denominators, such as ⅓ and ¼.

V

Variables Letters or symbols used to represent unknown quantities in equations. See unknowns.

Variable rate Loan in which interest goes up and down with the prevailing rates over the period of the loan. An example, commonly used in real estate today, is the adjustable rate mortgage, ARM.

Vertical analysis Method of financial statement analysis in which each major item is expressed as a percent of an important comparison base, such as net sales or total assets.

Volume The measurement of a three-dimensional object; measured in cubic units, such as cubic inches or cubic centimeters.

Volume = length × width × height.

W

Wage Compensation for services, usually on an hourly or daily basis.

Weighted average A modified method of calculating the arithmetic mean, whereby weights or indications of relative importance are assigned to the values being averaged.

Whole number Any number, 0 or greater, which does not contain a fraction or decimal. Also known as an integer.

For example 7, 84, and 200 are whole numbers.

Withholdings Amounts that are subtracted from an employees' gross earnings, such as federal income tax, social security tax, and medicare tax. Also known as payroll deductions.

Working capital The dollar amount of current assets financed with long-term debt on owner's equity.

Working capital = current assets − current liabilities.

Y

Yield The percent representing the annual return on an investment. Also known as return on investment, ROI.

Yield = annual income ÷ amount of investment.